Financial disclaimer

The following information is provided as an information service only and, therefore, does not constitute, and should not be relied upon as, financial product advice. None of the information provided takes into account your personal objectives, financial situation or needs, and you will need to make your own decision about how to proceed.

Alternatively, for financial product advice that takes account of your particular objectives, financial situation or needs, you should consider seeking financial advice from an Australian Financial Services licensee before making a financial decision.

E.T.H.I.C.A.L
Property Investing

The busy professional's guide to
double digit returns from
affordable and sustainable homes

Dr Dionne Payn

Book cover designed by Luke Harris,
Working Type Book Design.

ISBN:
Paperback: 978-0-6454461-0-4
Ebook: 978-0-6454461-1-1

I dedicate this book to my Mom and my Nan.
Both women of resilience, perseverance,
and commitment to service which I am very glad
rubbed off on me.

Contents

Transforming lives through property investment. A true story*.

Life — here's a summary of where I started getting it wrong and a snapshot of how I got it right.

I don't know about you, but when I was growing up, I always equated doing good and helping others with struggle. Maybe it's because we didn't have much, but what we had we tried to share with others. Whenever there was spare time, clothing, food, or money, we gave it back to our neighbours and the people in need in our community. For me, it meant growing up with a strong 'service' ethic, but there was also this link in my mind between giving back and never getting our heads far enough above water to feel comfortable. It wasn't until I grew up and had a family of my own, and then found my way into property investing through a rather circuitous route, that I realised I had it all wrong.

The truth is, you can do good and make money at the same time. Yes, it takes a highly developed blend of intent, process, people and commitment, but it really is possible.

You might already be feeling a bit cynical at this early juncture. Good, it means you're a critical thinker. But can I get you to read that section in bold one more time and let the truth of it sink in. And I know that once you see the big picture in writing, you'll recognise it for what it is — common sense. That realisation was a bit of a revelation to me at the time, and it changed my life. I hope it will change yours too.

Before lives are transformed, let's get acquainted — a little bit about you.

You may already know that you can grow wealth through property, even though you aren't achieving the income you need.

You may be seeing the challenges associated with our current housing models — including spiralling prices and lack of options for the vulnerable — and feel called to make a difference, but don't know how.

You may be making ethical choices in other areas of your life and want to do so through investing in property as well, but you feel torn between wanting to make a good return on your investment and investing in a socially responsible way. Am I close?

...and now a little about me — and my introduction to the property market.

> *Making money is important and doing more good for people is fulfilling... achieving both of these ends through ethical property investments is transformative and rewarding — for everyone!*

My name is Dr Dionne Payn and I am the Founder and CEO of High Impact Property Investments. I've always had a passion for helping people, initially through providing medicines for better health, and now by helping to create safe, secure and affordable homes where people can thrive.

In my previous career I was a research scientist, having completed my PhD thesis on medicinal natural products from sugarcane. After having our two children and becoming a stay-at-home Mum, my husband and I found ourselves in an interesting predicament: we couldn't afford to buy a home in the area we loved on one income.

Our solution was to seek creative ways to enter the property market, and we ended up working with a Joint Venture partner to renovate and subdivide a property in Northern NSW, Australia. He had cash but no time, and we had buckets of time but little cash, so it was a smart and productive partnership. At the end of that project, we'd all made money, and I had well and truly caught the property bug.

We completed two more small lot subdivision and renovation projects gaining experience and making money along the way. However, the highlight of my property journey was the development of 14 one-bedroom townhouses, again with Joint Venture partners. This was a project that provided affordable homes in a community where housing unafford-ability was a big issue. We made a great return as investors, but more importantly it was my first taste of investing in "property on purpose".

It was weird, but the feeling that I'd made a positive contri-bution to people's future was more rewarding even than the monetary returns. I'd always believed that just getting a job you loved and working hard would be fulfilling, but the reality was that I still felt as though there was something missing. Being able to participate in that venture generated that sense of fulfilment I'd been looking for, and I was keen to repeat the experience.

A major discovery.

That initial affordable homes development inspired me to explore more deeply the idea of transforming lives through property, with a focus on 4 avenues of opportunity:

1. *Creating affordable housing.*

2. *Sustainable properties (including commercial interests).*

3. *Designed and constructing Specialised Disability Accom-modation (SDA).*

4. *Building resilient communities.*

Evidence from research led me to the fact that it makes good economic sense to invest in homes that people can afford, ("affordable" is defined as being 30% or less of your annual income). When we do that, the buyers are then free to use their remaining income to thrive and keep our communities growing.

In addition, I learned that as a society we save money when we invest in properties that give more than they take. For example, when we:

✓ **position** our homes in a way that uses free energy from the sun and wind to heat and cool the home;

✓ **utilise** sustainable materials that are quick to regenerate, are not finite and therefore remain at an affordable price;

✓ **build** with materials that are healthy and don't cause disease for the people that live there, therefore saving on medical costs.

If you (re)search long and hard enough for bad news, eventually you'll find it but the key is to keep an eye out for impactful solutions too.

I found that there is a real need to build homes for people living with disabilities — homes genuinely designed and built for their lives and lifestyles rather than (often shabbily) put together by developers keen to take advantage of the cascades of NDIS funding issuing from government sources.

Finally, it became clear that when we build resilient communities, it means that when disaster and tragedy happen (think the triple whammy of floods in 2017, bushfires in 2018, and

COVID-19 from 2020), we can get back on our feet quickly because we are helping each other.

But the biggest surprise and most energising aspect of my investigation was that not only can we make these transformative improvements to the lives of many, when done properly, the returns for investors can be well into double digits.

I had found the magical combination of making money and making a difference, and it changed my life.

Realising that collaboration with other like-minded people was the way forward, in early 2021 I founded High Impact Property Investments with my then business partner at the time, Symon Peters. Together we have some 40 years of experience in the property development industry and Symon facilitated the development of almost 1,000 properties with a value approaching $500 million.

Now, I am on a mission to raise $1 billion for ethical property investments by December 2026.

By the time you read this, I'll have less than five years to achieve my goal, but I go into the task with a lot of confidence. Why? Because I understand the road ahead.

Some of the developers we'll need to complete such a huge undertaking are already onboard, fully vetted for relevant experience and, more significantly, to ensure that they're on the same page ethically and as far as our objectives go.

But there's still a lot of work to be done to ensure we have enough of the right people onboard. And my success in helping investors identify and get involved with projects that meet their intentions and desired outcomes, is a matter of record. I've also learned that the key to success is complete transparency and accountability, and I've put the systems in place to deliver it.

So, we're looking for investors who share our commitment to ethical investing and want to be part of the solution by aligning their investments with their values, but also aspire to benefit from double digit returns.

But this book is not an advertisement for my company (well, maybe a little bit). I am writing this so you can undertake the journey yourself if you think you're up for it.

This book is about giving you the tools and learning from my experience, how you can "Grow Wealth, Make an Impact and Leave A Legacy" through ethical property investing.

It was high time this book was written because of the times we're living in.

As I write this towards the end of 2021, many areas across Australia are experiencing a property boom. Again, let's look at the evidence:

+ *There's mass migration from the capital cities into south-east Queensland and regional areas of New South Wales, as well as other parts of Australia.*

✦ Both land and homes are in short supply.

✦ People are jumping, en masse, on the property bandwagon because they don't want to miss out or get left behind.

✦ As a result of all this, many are running on emotion rather than thinking rationally, and are at risk of making poor investment decisions.

What does this mean? It means there's a perfect storm of shortages driving up demand, buyers acting on FOMO (fear of missing out) and, in the middle of it all, some sharp-eyed and perhaps less than scrupulous developers taking advantage of the chaos. The vulnerable — single mothers, people living with disabilities, and others caught in the cycle of poverty and rising rents — are the ones getting left behind.

It has to be all about helping people.

The social impact we can bring through ethical property investing is well explained through the lens of Maslow's hierarchy of needs. When we provide affordable, sustainable and disability inclusive homes, we meet the physiological need for shelter, we go a long way towards meeting the need for safety and security, and we set the scene for the pursuit of the higher needs.

1. Maslow's Hierachy of Needs

Imagine the change that a person enduring homelessness experiences when moving from an environment where they lack basic protection, privacy and safety to something better. Or when a person living with disability moves into a home where they can fully access everything the home has to offer.

This is the change that high impact property investments can bring. Providing affordable, sustainable and disability inclusive homes gives inhabitants the space to build fulfilling relationships and have a sense of belonging within the community.

Your investment in these homes builds self-esteem and self-worth for the inhabitants — feelings that it's almost impossible to cultivate when a person is:

✓ at risk of or experiencing homelessness

✓ spending a large percentage of their income on heating and cooling and experiencing the stress that their predicament creates

✓ going without because there are parts of the property that they cannot access because it isn't set up to accommodate their physical abilities

Providing affordable, sustainable and disability inclusive homes enables people to be creative and reach their full potential in life.

Getting involved with an organisation that is making a difference is one way that we can overcome feelings of helplessness, guilt and even shame for the privileges that we have. Joining forces with others committed to making a bigger impact is a powerful act and improves our chances of success.

But is it a wise investment? Good question. Here's a straight answer.

The premise is that through ethical property investing, you can build your own wealth and contribute to building the collective wealth of society. All you need is the right process, partners and investors.

We're here to bust the pervasive myth that you can't make money through investing in affordable homes, sustainable properties, Specialised Disability Accommodation, and building resilient communities.

We've distilled what we've learned in the process of creating property investments with the potential to transform lives into a simple 7 step process we call the ETHICAL Framework. It's a tried-and-true method we use to evaluate and manage the projects we share with our clients. The elements of the ETHICAL Framework, which will be discussed in detail in later chapters, and which will provide you with the intelligence you need to go ahead and create your own part of the solution, are:

- *Experience*

- *Track record*

- *High impact*

- *Investment risk*

- *Collaborators*

- *Alignment*

- *Legacy*

In the following pages, we'll look at what motivates you and what you need to make ethical investing work for you, and then we'll delve into deep detail around the process itself.

Page by page, you'll build an understanding of the why, how, when, what and with whom you can embark on an ethical property investment adventure that will yield results both financial and personal, that perhaps you thought was impossible until now.

Naturally, there are always risks when it comes to investing in property, and things can and do go wrong. But I can attest that when you use the ETHICAL Framework and stick to it, in my experience those risks can be significantly reduced.

It really is possible for you to build long term sustainable wealth while helping to create a more inclusive, liveable, community-minded and sustainable world — and I hope you're ready to do just that.

Let's get started!

Chapter 2.

This book is for you so let's start with... you.

Your hopes and dreams for your family, your desire to help create a better world, and finding ways to make it all happen with the least amount of stress and drama are powerful motivators.

In the time I've been working on ethical property investments, it has become obvious that there is no 'typical' investor with whom we work. We have access to literally thousands of investors and they come from every sort of background and current situation.

The one thing they have in common is that they are seeking an investment opportunity that ticks more than one box. In addition to being profitable, their investment must make a positive contribution to society. It must deliver a high impact, not just to the investor but to the community, and make the world a better place.

You're here because you've joined the growing ranks of people who can see that if there is going to be positive change in the world, it's up to people like us — individuals, families and groups — to make it happen. There's a global movement towards ensuring as many of life's transactions as possible have more broadly beneficial impacts than they have had in the past — a movement typified by the Buy One Give One (B1G1) initiative, businesses and individuals committing to the United Nations' Sustainable Development Goals, business becoming B Corps, and more. And making high impact property investments is about providing just those sorts of opportunities.

But this is not about suffering so that other people can improve their lives. Let's call it smart altruism — the kind where you benefit and your actions have positive conse-quences for others, without the need for anyone to deprive themselves along the way. So before we begin talking about how our ethical property investment system works, let's get some ground rules clear. Let's talk about what you need to get out of this.

I'll just blurt it out — you need your money to work for you. We all do.

As much as we're both here to make the world a better place, and to help people who don't have the same advantages we're currently enjoying, you and I simply can't afford to invest in projects that do not make money. That's the fast track to being on the receiving end of philanthropy, and neither of us wants that.

So the first criteria for any investments you make, including those in affordable and sustainable housing, SDA and building resilient communities, is that they must make money. Preferably good money — as in double digit returns.

After all, the cost of living is increasing. According to the Australian Bureau of Statistics (ABS) the Consumer Price Index (CPI) increased by 3.8% between June 2020 to June 2021. In that same period, wages grew by just 1.7%. As the gap between the cost of living and wages widens it becomes harder to meet rising living costs and save for retirement. A recent survey by the ABC Australia Talks podcast, found that out of over 50,000 respondents, 62% of them were worried that they didn't have enough to retire.

We are living longer than ever before, working longer hours and for more years than in previous generations. We want to be able to invest our money in a way that means our money is working for us, instead of having to work so hard. And that's what I want for you too, but I am offering you a unique pathway to that result.

Through ethical property investing you can grow your wealth and feel good about making a difference.

Is ethical property investment profitable?

Now, you may have trouble getting your head around the idea that investing in the kind of projects I am advocating can bear rewarding returns. Your mind is probably popping with the kind of questions I get asked all the time:

1. *When you build affordable housing, if you're charging rent low enough to be affordable for those on low incomes, how can it be profitable?*

2. *Building sustainable living homes is expensive — you need solar panels, double glazing and other costly fittings. How can you make money out of that?*

3. *Why should I care anyway when traditional property investment has served me so well up to now?*

The answers to the first two questions are simple but complex. The simple answer is, I know that investing in ethical building projects can yield high returns, because I have done it over and over again. The complex answer is, it requires:

+ *meticulous planning*

+ *intense attention to detail*

+ *partners who share your commitment to making a difference*

+ *background knowledge around the market you're targeting*

+ *awareness of the various governmental assistance packages available*

+ *demand (and need) for the product you're planning in the area you're considering*

The one bit of proof that I can give you that this sector is profitable is that in the last few years I have seen a great many developers and their investors getting involved in it. Sadly, some of these developers are interested solely in profit, and to maximise their returns they cut corners, don't invest sufficiently in design and fitout to create the most positive environment for the residents, and generally give our industry a bad name.

These wolves wouldn't be there unless the sector was profitable, but the way they approach it makes me sad. That's one of the main reasons I started High Impact Property Investments — because I wanted to prove that you can create homes that really do transform peoples' lives and still make excellent returns, without resorting to cheap or inadequate solutions. And I can show you the proof.

As far as question three goes, I can't answer that for you — it's something you'll have to decide for yourself. But I can tell you that the first step is to open your mind to the possibility that you can achieve double digit returns through ethical property investing. Once you do that, you will start to see the myriad of opportunities that are already available.

In any case, I believe that if you've read this far, you've already answered question three yourself. You're here because you do care, and you're already committed to putting your money to good use, both for yourself and for the society we all share.

I've never met an investor who didn't want their money to work for them — most need it to do so, because as mentioned above, it's about making sure their future is comfortable and not reliant on the ever-shrinking pension. As an example of the kind of investors I do meet, let me introduce you to 'Zahra' and Audrey:

Zahra and Audrey

Zahra is a single mum with three energetic children. She has a chronic health condition, which means that she can't work full-time. Zahra recently received an inheritance and wanted to know how she could make her money work for her.

When I spoke to Zahra about the work that we do at High Impact Property investments, she was fascinated. "I need my money to work for me, but I really want to know how I can do that in a way that I can feel good about," she said. "I can't work full-time anymore and I have to be responsible with this gift. It has to outlast me and be able to provide for my family when I'm gone".

In Zahra's case, needing to get the best return was important to her. She wanted to enjoy a good quality of life but her health challenges meant that working full-time wasn't going to work for her or her family. Achieving passive income through property investing was a high priority for her so she could focus on her recovery and on being the best Mum she could be to her children.

Then there was Audrey, who decided to invest in one of our affordable housing projects because she saw it as an opportunity to get her foot on the first rung of the housing ladder. Knowing the difference between things like long-term leases, energy efficient design and appliances, and proximity to schools, shops and transport can make to the residents, she was eager to see her money used for such a positive purpose.

Today, Audrey is a living example of the kind of returns that can be achieved through ethical property investments and importantly, she and her family can live in comfort and confidence.

Aligning your investment choices with your values leaves a lasting legacy.

The only constant is change and the only question is, "if you don't like it, what are you prepared to do about it?"

The world is changing. People everywhere are starting to realise that change for the better doesn't just happen — we have to make it happen. Ever since economist Milton Friedman wrote a paper entitled "The Social Responsibility of Business is to Increase its Profits"[1] in 1970, it has become increasingly obvious that the corporations that supply most of our daily needs cannot be relied upon to allow the good of society or the planet to interfere with the pursuit of profit. Today's CEOs feel justified in doing whatever it takes to make money for its shareholders, and literally nothing else matters. The good ones keep within the rules, but the rules are often cast in their favour, and don't make principled actions necessary.

But we the people are discovering that we have a power over those corporations, and we can compel them to act in socially, environmentally and ethically responsible ways, by threatening the profits they chase. By withholding our custom until they do so, we can ensure that businesses act in socially, environmentally and civically responsible ways — and it's working.

According to Nielsen's 2015 Global Corporate Sustainability Report, 66% of consumers are willing to pay extra to buy products or brands from companies known for their commitment to social and environmental impact[2]. That number increased to 73% among the millennial demographic.

In data collected by Nuveen in its "Third Annual Responsible Investing Survey"[3], 90% of millennials reported that they would prefer to work for a company that had a positive social and environmental impact on the world, compared to 70% of non-millennials. In the same survey, 92% of millennials reported they cared more about having a positive impact on society than doing well financially."

In an era when "brand" is so important to the profits of a corporation, having a brand that resonates with the values and principles of its consumers is becoming more and more important, and it's changing the way companies pursue profits.

Millennials are leading the charge in working for, buying from, or investing in companies that share their values when it comes to social and environmental issues.

When we knowingly invest in ventures and enterprises that do not align with our values, we feel uncomfortable. We know that we are falling short of our own standards, and our actions are having an impact that we don't want. The danger in not being open to the possibility of ethical property investing is that we keep the inequalities in our society and the destruction of the environment in place, which ultimately affects us all.

Consider the story of Janet.

Janet is a professional speaker and coach who makes conscious choices in many aspects of her life, such as eating organic foods, using natural medicines and minimising the use of plastic where she can in her day-to-day life. As a single mum with two boys under 10, she renovated her home two years ago to include solar panels and a battery system, LED lights and a grey water system to minimise her household water use.

One day she was looking at her investment portfolio and realised that some of the companies she was investing in were not in alignment with her values. Through a managed investment fund, she was investing in tobacco and coal mining operations, which she would never knowingly have chosen to do. This was a bit of a shock for her, as it was the first time she had considered the industries that her money was being invested into, and she didn't want to support companies that she believed were harmful to human health or to the planet.

Janet realised that she needed to find a way to invest that not only aligned with her values but also matched or exceeded the level of income that she was already receiving from those investments. She wanted to have peace of mind knowing that her money was working for her in ways that matched who she was as an informed, conscious consumer.

I am guessing that, like Janet, you're starting to question how we can make more ethical choices in our lives. Whether it is choosing to reduce the amount of plastic we use, being more deliberate about not supporting the fast fashion industry or switching to hybrid / electric vehicles, there is increased awareness that we can make a difference based on how we choose to spend our money.

What this means for you in the ethical property investment context.

We are the generation that will finally stand up and say that it is no longer enough to sit by and watch the:

- ✦ *affordable housing crisis escalate*

- ✦ *inequalities that people with disabilities face, continue to divide us*

- ✦ *climate crisis unfold*

We will no longer accept that it's "just the way it is," or, "it's the Government's responsibility to do something about that."

Pulitzer Prize winning author, Alice Walker famously said, "The most common way people give up their power is by thinking they don't have any." We all have the power to take action in some way and investing in projects and initiatives that align with our values is one of the most powerful ways we can make a difference.

If you know where to look, there is:

- ✓ An impressive array of creative solutions that provide affordable rental or owner-occupied homes — solutions that also yield excellent returns for investors.

- ✓ An increasing number of architects, developers and builders are designing and building homes that use resources efficiently in both the construction and the ongoing running of the home. These homes are designed to be energy- and water-efficient, to use space wisely, and to be comfortable and inviting places to live.

✓ Tremendous progress being made in the design and construction of SDA (specialist disability accommodation) homes which ultimately provide more freedom and quality of life for people with disabilities.

But, as I mentioned above, not everyone is in this business for honourable reasons. You need to be on the lookout for projects that are more about greenwashing or social washing — providing a veneer of environmental and social responsibility without any substance and using disinformation to make them seem more principled than they actually are — than genuinely meeting the needs of the vulnerable.

We all see examples of this every day, such as when companies label their products as "green" or "natural", or place images on their products that suggest that they contain ingredients that are eco-friendly when in reality they are not.

In the property investment industry, the words "affordable" and "sustainable" are sometimes used without reference to what they mean. The lack of transparency around these terms and the projects to which they pertain makes it hard to trust whether organisations truly have the interests of all the stakeholders at heart — in some cases it is just marketing BS.

Unfortunately, this can even lead to the suspicion that genuinely environmentally and socially responsible property projects are not profitable, based on the notion that the people who create these projects may have lots of compassion and empathy but lack the business acumen to obtain good financial returns. There's a fallacy that only hard-nosed operators can generate good returns in property, and those hard-nosed types probably don't care about developing socially responsible properties that make a difference to people and the planet.

Thankfully, the hard-nosed developer stereotype is becoming less common and there are many developers and organisations that are creating ethical property projects on a large scale. A prime example is the 360 Collective, one of our developer partners who, as I write, are creating a 72-bed affordable housing project in South-East Queensland. For investors, these types of projects not only provide an opportunity to be financially rewarded but additionally, they create a more meaningful outcome where the investor can feel fulfilled knowing that they have made a lasting difference in their community and our society at large.

Ask the right questions (and know the right answers).

The art of getting to the truth of a matter is knowing what it looks and sounds like. Remember, almost all gold prospectors know what gold looks like before they go searching for it.

How can you be sure that the project you're considering investing in truly aligns with your values?

First, it pays to have a clear and explicit answer to the question, "what are your values?" Start by thinking about three further questions:

1. *What do you want for this world and how you can contribute to it?*

2. *What kind of moral environment would you like to nurture in your home?*

3. *What kinds of actions are you willing to take to improve our global community?*

Write down your beliefs, your wishes for the world and what you're prepared to do to help them come about.

Now that you have a handle on your values, apply them to the project you're considering. Ask these 8 pertinent questions that will help you determine the actual principles of the people involved, and whether they meet your criteria:

1. *What is your (the developer's) definition of affordable housing, and for whom are these houses to be affordable?*

2. *What metrics do you use for the sustainability of a home?*

3. *What materials are you using, and what energy-saving and environmentally friendly measures will you be including in the building process and the finished homes themselves?*

4. *Are you offering long term leases?*

5. *What level of needs do these SDA homes cater for (some occupants will require high levels of support while others, to varying degrees, will not), and do you have a clear pathway to getting tenants for these homes?*

6. *Will the homes conform to Green Star design principles, and will they be Green Star rated?*

7. *Will the homes be Nationwide House Energy Rating Scheme (NatHERS) assessed, and how many NatHERS stars are you aiming for?*

8. *Will these homes sit well with the existing community?*

You can read up on what the ratings systems mentioned in points 6 and 7 mean at **Green Star Rating System | Green Building Council of Australia (gbca.org.au)** and **Nationwide House Energy Rating Scheme (NatHERS)** respectively. There, you can also research the kinds of materials and actions that are environmentally friendly and energy-saving, to help you make sense of the answers you get.

But the bottom line is, if the developer can deliver hard facts, design details and planned living outcomes that comply with your requirements and agree with the values you have articulated, the investment you're considering is most likely genuinely ethical.

To sum up the advantages and opportunities...

The business we're in isn't an outlier — it's a mainstream, highly regarded and increasingly popular investment option.

It gives people like you the opportunity to align your invest-ment choices with your values and helps you to live those values. Yes, there are pitfalls, and yes, if you strike out on your own, you're in for a steep learning curve. But that's why you're here — to take advantage of the experience I've gath-ered and to avoid making the kind of mistakes I had to make to get where I am.

Getting started can be the hardest part — here's how to start.

Karen is a successful property investor in her sixties. She's very community minded and does a lot for other people, often volunteering her time at the local soup kitchen. In addition, Karen is an active member of the CWA and donates money to local causes.

The impact that the affordable housing crisis is having on friends and other members of her community is very clear to Karen. One of her friends Anne, was widowed after her husband passed away from cancer, and she wanted to down-size from their family home. The trouble was, Anne didn't have enough money to buy a new property — the recent property boom had priced everything in the area out of her range.

Determined to help Anne, as they'd lived in the same area for many years, Karen wanted to keep her close by so she could continue to provide support for her friend. So she searched for suitable accommodation for Anne to rent, going to rental property inspections, often with 50 to 60 other people at the same inspection. She found it almost impossible to find somewhere suitable for Anne, and often when she did, she was outbid by somebody that could pay more rent, 12 months in advance.

Given Karen's experience in property investing, she didn't think it would be so hard to find something, but as she later lamented, "I want to help by providing affordable housing myself but I just don't know how it can be done when property prices have gone through the roof."

That is a whole lot of context and I am guessing that, like Karen, you see these and other social issues that are happening in your suburb, your town, your state and our country, and you want to help but don't know how. Whether it's the affordable housing crisis, the climate emergency, or the challenge of rebuilding communities after disaster, as humans we're hardwired to help. But sometimes the issues just feel too big, too complex and too tragic. We become overwhelmed and we don't even know where or how to start.

Thankfully, it is easy to get behind people that take the lead. Keep in mind, comedienne Celeste Barber's crowd fundraising campaign. When the world was seeing horrifying images of Australia on fire back in the summer of 2019, Celeste set a goal to raise $30,000 for the Rural Fire Service, but instead $51 million in donations poured in from concerned citizens all across the world.

Most of us aren't set up to take on a leadership role like Celeste, but we're eager to follow someone like her when they provide that direction and inspiration. You may not know it, but in the realm of the affordable and SDA housing markets, that leadership has already arisen. The need has been identified and quantified, and there are elements within both the public and private sectors that are setting the goals and providing the pathways. All you need to do is find them and choose who you want to work with.

Ours is an industry set for growth and here are the numbers that count.

+ *There will be a need for 650,000 affordable or social housing homes in Australia nationally over the next 15 years according to a recent University of New South Wales (UNSW) Futures Research Centre report.*

+ *Federal and State Governments have committed funds to tackle the issue.*

+ *In 2020, the Victorian Government committed $5.3 billion for affordable and social housing, while the NSW Government has committed $2.3 billion.*

+ *The Federal Government pledged $1.6 billion through the National Housing and Homelessness Agreement (NHHA).*

Despite this, experts predict that the amounts committed will fall short of their target and the result could be many more people slipping through the cracks.

This is an opportunity for private investors.

It seems clear that private investment will be required to provide funding to meet the funding needs not met by the government. The Australian Financial Review (AFR) reported that superannuation funds will be one of the major players when it comes to funding the shortfall in social and afford-able housing[4]. In light of this, it's not surprising that First State Super recently launched an affordable housing project for key workers in Melbourne[5] and Aware Super have invested almost $800 million into affordable housing projects for Sydney based key workers[6].

Sustainability is becoming popular.

There is a growing trend towards investing in the design and construction of more sustainable homes as well. In May 2021, the National Housing Finance and Investment Corporation (NHFIC) issued $343 million dollars' worth of sustainability bonds and were massively oversubscribed[7]. The bonds have provided funds for Community Housing Provider CHL to create commercial properties and social housing that include energy efficiency, renewable energy and rainwater harvesting for toilet flushing and landscaping. The bonds which are paying 2.35% p.a. over 15 years, attracted investors from Australia and overseas, demonstrating that there are plenty of ethically minded fund managers that want to make a difference.

Growth in the NDIS sector is unprecedented.

Impact investing is also playing a role in NDIS housing, with fund managers from organisations such as Australian Unity, Macquarie Group and Inspire Impact having placed $650 million into funding for almost 1000 NDIS participants[8]. These fund managers predict that the sector could be worth $12 billion dollars over the next 5 years with good governance

Social Housing Need to 2036
- 685 - 5,000
- 5,001 - 10,000
- 10,001 - 15,000
- 15,001 - 23,058

Adelaide   Brisbane   Hobart

Melbourne   Perth   Sydney

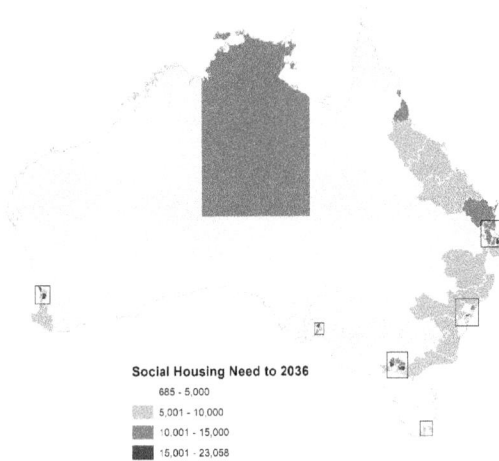

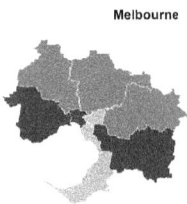

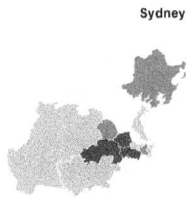

2. Affordable Housing Requirements in Australia by 2036

and more transparency in place by the National Disability Insurance Agency (NDIA).

This is where you come in.

While all this demonstrates the enormous potential of the market we're involved in, there's no way we should leave investing into affordable homes, sustainable properties and SDA homes to the big super funds. Ethical investors like you will have a crucial role and space to play in providing homes that meet the needs of a diverse section of the community. The start has been made, the examples are there, and the field is wide open. And the good news is that if you get involved, you can be very well rewarded for it.

Are double digit returns really possible?

When we think of new homes being built, the first image that springs to mind is your typical suburban 3-4 bedroom home, with a backyard and double garage or at least two car parking space. If you're an inner-city dweller, your first thought may be of the swathes of two-bedroom apartment complexes that abound in our cities.

The demand for housing is changing shape.

However, the way we live is changing, with an increase in the number of single person households from 19% — 24% between 1986 to 2016[9]. At the same time, only 5.6% of homes in Australia had 1 bedroom, which means many in that demographic may be paying for more space than they actually need. Not only that, in the period 2011 — 2016, dwellings with no or one bedroom were the slowest growing category, with the largest growth occurring in the four-bedroom home category[10].

In addition, according to the NDIS, as at 21 December 2021, of some 18,361 people across Australia who were SDA-eligible, 3,857 did not live in an SDA residence or were seeking an alternative[11]. Considering that there were 4.4 million people in Australia living with a disability in 2018[12], the demand for specialist disabled accommodation is highly likely to keep on growing.

Clearly, the need for affordable housing, sustainable properties, resilient communities and providing homes for people with disabilities is not going away anytime soon. This represents a massive opportunity to use our money to make a bigger impact, and create a better world for ourselves, our families and future generations.

How it works.

There are multiple approaches we can take to investing in properties for the growing number of people who need affordable, sustainable and/or specialist housing. As noted above, there is a shortfall of single bed properties, and these can be incorporated into high density designs.

However, one increasingly popular way of providing affordable housing is through co-living — a housing model in which three or more unrelated people share a dwelling that provides a mixture of private and shared spaces. The benefits of co-living include comfort, affordability, and a greater sense of belonging. The co-living trend is becoming more prevalent as rental affordability decreases.

A living example of how it works in real life.

Our first High Impact Property Investment was with a developer who designed a dual key property, essentially a four-bedroom house split into two separate halves, with two bedrooms, a kitchen, living and dining room on either side of a dividing wall. Each bedroom had its own ensuite bathroom, and the project was designed to provide four women over 55 an opportunity to rent an affordable property.

With bills included in the rent, energy efficiency was an essential design requirement, and the addition of a photovoltaic system and batteries provided insulation against rising energy costs.

The backyard was designed as a shared space for the four residents. This mixture of private and shared space allows areas for private retreat as well as more community living. The benefit of co-living done in this way is it fosters a sense of companionship and belonging in which we as humans can thrive.

Note: Delivering properties fully furnished gives some protection from damage from multiple people moving their furniture, but also makes it easier for tenants to move straight into the property.

One of the challenges that face women over 55 in private rental accommodation, is the lack of security of tenure. We commonly hear from women who have moved into a rental property on a short-term lease and then have to move again once the lease has expired. Moving house can be a costly exercise when you take into account truck hire, downtime from paid employment and the costs to reinstate services.

It was therefore important to us that the developer offered long-term leases, so that the residents felt more secure in the property. The upside for investors is that long term leases are valuable, as they mean that vacancy rates are reduced, and long-term rent is assured.

In this particular project the return on capital to investors was 12% per annum.

Specialist Disability Accommodation.

Providing Specialist Disability Accommodation (SDA) homes is an emerging investment opportunity which also provides double digit returns when working with the right develop-ment team. One of our developer colleagues is building SDA homes in the outer suburbs of Sydney. Using the complying development code (a fast-track way to obtain development approvals in NSW), these SDA properties are brought from level site to lock-up in just 55 days.

The rewards.

Investing into these types of projects yields triple bottom line results. Not only do the financial returns make sense, but there is also the satisfaction and peace of mind that as an investor you are investing in partnership with, rather than at the expense of others.

Investing in this way generates more sustainable wealth. When we invest in these types of projects, we can use our returns to invest more and to serve more people. This creates an upwards spiral effect — the people we serve can also serve more people. I believe it is in this way that we can create positive change in our society and create a world worth living in.

Let's finish this part with another story.

When Charles was young, his parents were advised to purchase an investment property, which was probably the wrong advice for them at the time. Interest rates increased — this was during the 80's and interest rates peaked at 17% — and they weren't able to get regular tenants for the property, and ended up having to sell the property at a loss, losing a lot of money in the process. Sadly, they never recovered. They are now in their seventies, on a government pension, with nothing else to their names.

Charles was determined that this wasn't going to happen to him. He became an accountant and has educated himself in investing. He now has a diverse investments portfolio building a tidy nest-egg.

Later on, Charles heard a podcast where one of our team members was talking about how we help investors achieve double digit returns through ethical property investing. He was particularly captivated with the idea of helping women over 55 into affordable rentals and doing this with a group that had a proven track record of success.

After booking a conversation with the team, Charles became a member of the High Impact Property Investment Network (which gives investors exclusive access to these kinds of projects) and was then making 12% per annum on his investment.

He feels good that he's making a difference with his money and that his investment played a part in making a positive impact on the lives of four women who, in the current housing market, may not have had an opportunity to have an affordable rental property.

Charles is just one example of what we have proven many times — that there are ways to make double digit returns through ethical property investing, as long as you are willing to apply creative solutions and let go of the idea of sticking to what you have always done.

To wrap it all up

You're here because you've independently come to the conclusion that investing in property doesn't have to be a zero-sum game, where there are winners and losers. Your ethical standards have developed to a point where you're keen to use your money, and your buying choices to affect some good in this crazy but loveable world of ours. You're not alone — millions around the world have come to similar conclusions, and people are starting to realise that we, the consumers, can persuade companies to do the right thing by the environment and the community, simply through the choices we make.

But wanting to make a positive difference and finding honourable and responsible ways to do it can be two different things. There are a lot of grey areas out there and unfortunately, there are still some who would take advantage of your good intentions, without delivering on glib promises. Not only that, it's easy to feel powerless in the face of seemingly insurmountable problems such as the affordable housing and climate crises.

However, finding and working with organisations that have already proven that they share your values and are already delivering solutions to these issues, is a good way to make an impact in our communities and society at large.

Moving away from investing in destructive industries and placing your investment funds into projects that are deliberately designed to help people and the planet to thrive, is a powerful statement. This win-win way of property investing is an answer to many of the challenges we face on a global scale and is the legacy that we can leave for future generations.

The benefits of ethical property investment are far-reaching and can be achieved through a variety of projects. There is an abundance of opportunities available to grow wealth through providing affordable homes, sustainable properties, building resilient communities and inclusive homes for people with disabilities, without having to choose between doing good or making a profit.

The choice you now face is whether to go it alone and create your own path — which is what this book is all about — or join with others who have already learned the lessons you'll find in these pages. Either way, I hope and believe that this book will be useful to you. If you go it alone, you'll find these insights invaluable. If you choose to join with others who have already proven their commitment to ethical property investing, these pages will help you understand the process, and ask the vital questions that will make it all make sense.

Now we come to the core part of this book, the ETHICAL framework. It will give you the tools to do your due diligence, from gaining experience and education, to ensuring that your collaborators share your values and the proposed project is aligned with them. There's a fair bit of technical detail and quite a lot to take on board, but at the end of it, you'll be ready to pursue a rewarding ethical property investment practice. Let's do it together.

For a special video relating to this section visit:
https://www.hipi.global/book/intro

SCAN ME

The ETHICAL Framework — your insurance policy for success

Good things come to those who plan, and plans are based on strategic frameworks that agree with, align to and/or promote your values, aspirations and vision. In short, you will need a framework to support your goals.

Here's where we dive into the deep end of ethical investing. I developed this framework myself to help me — and now you — make decisions about which projects, project partners, outcomes and processes I would use to drive my company, High Impact Property Investments.

3. *The ETHICAL Framework*

Here's what "high impact" actually means to me and what it could mean for — and others.

As an aside here, I am sure that by now you've already deduced that the term "high impact" refers primarily to the effect the investment has on the end user — it provides them with affordable and/or sustainable housing, or it gives a person living with a disability the opportunity to live in an environment that allows them to make full use of all the facilities and amenities that most of us take for granted. But the "high impact" is also for the investor, too. We aim for — and have so far achieved — double digit returns for our investors, while at the same time attaining the high impact outcomes the end users will enjoy.

The corollary to the term "high impact" is "legacy". Participating in a high impact property investment allows you to leave a legacy of positive contribution to the community. That means one day you can look back on your investment history and say to yourself, "you know, that was one amazing experience. I made a measurable difference in the lives of a bunch of people I'll probably never meet, and gave them the space, the time and the opportunity to realise their own potential. Maybe — hopefully — one or more of the people I helped will in turn help to make the world a better place themselves. And I made money while I was doing all that. That's something to be proud of."

Sorry, just a little diversion there but I'm sure you'll agree, an important one. Achieving a high impact and creating a meaningful legacy is what my team is all about, and I hope it will become what you're all about too.

Who is the ETHICAL framework for?

The ETHICAL Framework is specifically suited to syndicate investing. That is, a group of people putting money together to invest in a property development project in order to obtain worthy returns on their investment.

Syndicate investing is useful because it:

✓ enables you to participate in projects that you wouldn't ordinarily be able to fund or take the time to manage yourself.

✓ offers you scope to be involved in projects that have a greater outcome for a higher number of people (i.e. both the investors and the eventual residents).

✓ allows you to take advantage of the security a group investment offers, as well as to leverage off the experience of the people involved.

The last point there is particularly useful and comforting if you're new to property investing as you will have that peace of mind that comes with working towards a goal along with those that are experienced in this area.

Here's how the ETHICAL framework works.

The aim of the framework is to give you a point-by-point basis for assessing the various aspects of each potentially high impact property investment you're considering. It gives you the structure and background you need to examine the projected impact of the project from both your own financial standpoint and from the social and environmental impact it will have, and whether or not it meets your other non-financial criteria.

Your first task will be to honestly establish your level of experience — which will be vital in selecting which projects to get involved in. We'll show you how to grade the track record of the developer and assess their credentials as leaders of the projects. That's important because in the section C is for Collaborators, you'll find out just how many diverse people and groups will be required to make the project a success

— from real estate agents and architects to engineers, builders, property managers and financial controllers — and it's crucial that the developer has the skills and capacity to bring all those collaborators together.

There's a lot to explore, so together we'll be helping you establish:

- ✦ *what you expect from the investment*
- ✦ *whether it suits your risk profile (which we'll guide you in determining)*
- ✦ *whether the project and the people involved truly align with your values*
- ✦ *what the legacy from your involvement will be*

We've found that the projects that scored highly on each of the components in the ETHICAL framework stood the greatest chance of helping our clients to grow wealth, make an impact and leave a legacy. We know it works, and while it demands a fair bit of learning and attention to detail from you, if you follow the framework's precepts closely, it will help you achieve the success, the impact and the legacy you're seeking.

Chapter 4

E is for Experience.

If you commit to an ethical property investment, it's imperative that it's successful. Because while you're relying on your investment to earn money and help secure your future — which is important — the people who'll live in the homes you're planning, are in need of the lifechanging impacts your decisions enable. In a lot of cases, it's fair to say that your investment will help many people to have a much better future.

Remember when you were younger, maybe a university graduate, and you went out looking for a job. You quite likely finished up in that frustrating place where nobody would hire you because you didn't have any experience, and you couldn't get any experience because nobody would hire you.

The good news is, you're not quite in that position now. But you are probably lacking the kind of experience you'll need to be successful in the high impact property investment market. You need to learn, and learn quickly, how it all works, who's involved, and what can go wrong — as well as what can go right.

Let's do a quick reality check by asking, "what exactly is your experience?"

Before you begin, you need to make an honest appraisal of your current level of experience. I am assuming that you're a retail investor — that is, a "mum and dad investor" type who's using the equity in your home, or perhaps an inheritance or some other sum of money to secure the money you'll be putting into this type of investment.

Even if you have just one property investment behind you — maybe an investment property that you rent out, or a block you subdivided — you'll have a level of financial and practical literacy that will be of great assistance. Moving up into this type of investing helps you make the transition from retail to sophisticated investor and opens up a range of higher-earning opportunities for you — and the more experience you gain, the more opportunities will come your way.

If this is your first property investment venture, I'm afraid you have some learning to do, but that shouldn't put you off. It just means you need to tread a little more carefully. But if you keep on learning, you'll make money and the range of opportunities available to you will continue to grow.

The good news is, as a retail investor you're protected by laws, and through the activities of organisations like the Australian

Prudential Regulation Authority (APRA) and the Australian Securities and Investments Commission.

But the point here is not to dissuade you. The point is that you need to be candid about your level of experience and be ready to admit that you need help. Oh, and keep on gathering experience.

Even if you rate yourself as an experienced property investor, if this is your first foray into high impact property investing, I recommend you start with an education in this next level of property investment.

What's the story behind the numbers?

Every project has a story, and it begins with a question: what is the purpose of this project?

The answer (especially if it is a high impact investment) should be long and detailed, and tell you:

- *why the project has been proposed, and exactly what it entails*

- *where the development will be located, and why that area has been chosen*

- *who the target buyers and tenants are, and why they want to live there*

- *The key personnel involved in the project*

- *What security there is on invested funds*

+ *The exit strategy — is the property to be held for rental yields or sold?*

If it's a high impact investment, the answer will also include:

+ *what the outcomes for the residents will be*

+ *what positive contribution the project will make to the community*

+ *what the financial benefit to you will be.*

When you have that in front of you, it's a matter of determining whether there are solid numbers and facts to back the answers up. That is, you need to start with the proposed location: what's happening in the area? Do the people we want to attract live in that area, or want to live there? Will the property meet the needs of the target client? Does the area serve their needs, or is there an infrastructure plan that will make the location more desirable for residents by the time the project is complete or soon after?

Do you have an exit plan?

Hope for the best and (exit) plan for the worst. Wise words for weird times!

Not so long ago I was involved in a development in Northern New South Wales. I knew the market well and I also knew the development would appeal to young professionals and families looking for affordable homes in the area. We even had an offer, for one of the units, which we accepted, before we settled on the purchase of the property. So, we knew the strategy we wanted to employ, we had meetings, we made decisions, everything seemed to be falling into place, and we were keen to get started.

However, something big, unexpected and unstoppable came along and scuttled our plans. A pandemic started sweeping the world, and the market stalled. It was a very scary time for everyone, and people just, en masse, decided to sit back and wait to see what happened next.

I mention this because there's a crucial element to every plan, and that's the exit strategy. You need to know how you're going to extricate yourself from the project if unforeseen circumstances arise like a pandemic popping up, and when to recognise that you need to action your exit plan. In that particular case we were able to find someone to take over the purchase contract for the property. Yes, that sounds like a happy accident and I'm also aware that my blithe description of our solution might sound a bit flippant. The point is though, that we had identified another cash-rich buyer during the due diligence phase who had funds ready to go. Ensuring that we covered all the bases and making sure we ignored nothing during our due diligence phase meant that in the case of such a "black swan" event, our exit plan could be activated.

Go back to school.

As you can see from the above, when you move into larger scale property investing, which is what our high impact sector is all about, you need to understand what to look for in a good project and you need to have the tools to assess the skills of the management team and their history. You need to be able to interpret what they're telling you, and to separate the reality from the wildly optimistic or downright fabricated.

Too good to be true?

So often we hear that "if it sounds too good to be true, it probably is". But that's not necessarily true — note the judicious use of the world probably. And if you have the right level of financial literacy and experience in the area, you can tell the "sounds too good to be true because it is too good to be true" from the "sounds too good to be true but is actually true" opportunities. That's why it's so important to get the right education and the appropriate level of education in this discipline.

Now, there are a lot of different ways you can get that education, some better and more practical than others. And I have one that offers you a "learn on the job" approach.

Here's how best to "Learn as you Earn".

> *While in theory there's no difference between theory and practice, in practice there is. Remember that saying, it's the reason why on-the-job training is both precious and potentially precarious.*

Typically, when we think of learning something, it's a static process. You go and sit in a room and you do a course, and you learn how to do this thing. That's great except for the fact that when you learn in a classroom, you get all the theory, but you actually don't get the experience.

A lot of people like you, recognising the need for practical experience, are getting that education and experience "live", and earning money as they go, by joining a property investment syndicate.

Another reason why a syndicate is a good idea.

Taking on an ethical investment project is a major task. You need a well organised, clear and comprehensive business case. You need to know that the management team is on the ball. And you need to have good data to work with. If you don't have sufficient experience in property investing, you may not know how to conduct your own research — or even where to start — or undertake your due diligence into whether it's a good deal. Under those circumstances, it's hard to tell if the data you're being offered is actually reliable. Going it alone to try and pick up all that stuff can be really stressful, so it's no wonder to me that syndicate investing is on the rise.

Joining an ethical property investment syndicate is a bit like buying shares in a company, except you're sharing the profits of a property development. One of the biggest advantages of joining an investment syndicate is that for most of us it puts bigger, higher quality developments within our reach, and opens up the potential for better returns.

But for someone who wants to become more of a sophisticated investor (as opposed to a retail investor), it's much more than that. A syndicate gives you access to a network of people who've already learned a lot of the lessons involved, and who you can talk to and leverage their experience. If you choose the right group, one that offers a high degree of transparency and accountability, you'll receive detailed updates regularly and learn as you go. When anything crops up that you don't understand or agree with, you can bring it up with other members and get the benefit of their knowledge or talk to the syndicate managers about your questions and concerns.

When you understand the business model because it's been properly explained to you with examples of past projects, you feel comfortable. When the team that you're dealing with has the experience and skills you lack, it gives you peace of mind. There's trust in that relationship. And when you have the data to prove that it's a good decision, you can feel good about your decision. For a start, you won't second guess yourself and secondly you are much more likely to get a good result.

An unashamed plug.

I am a staunch advocate of people getting a practical education in the world of high impact property investments because, as the founder of my business (of the same name), I know that it works.

Given the absolute need to succeed from your first investment, my advice to you is, get at least one project under your belt with a syndicate and one important benefit from doing that is the education you'll gain by the experience.

Our "Learn as you Earn program."

4. One Of Our High Impact Property Investment Network meetings

In the last couple of years, we've had quite a number of inves-tors who have come in to take advantage of our "learn as you earn" model and earn excellent returns at the same time. In one recent example, we had a group who were keen to get into the commercial property sector and we worked with the developer to make that happen.

The project was the construction of one building designed to have five different tenancies. We were able to split those tenancies via strata subdivision, which then meant that each tenancy could be sold separately. And it made lucrative sense for it to work that way. Imagine the building as a cake — if you sell a whole cake, you sell it for one price, but if you sell parts of the cake, then you end up making more than you would if you just sell the cake.

And that's how we created five properties for sale, which minimised the risk and maximised the profits for each of the investors. They were present through the whole process, and they saw how it worked. To keep people informed we had:

- ✓ Regular Q&A webinars with the developers where they gave updates on the projects
- ✓ Interviews with the consultants and collaboration partners
- ✓ Regular networking events

And happily, the investors ended up earning a great return on their investments as well as a valuable education into the finer points of property development.

Let us match you with a project commensurate with your experience.

The smart thing about joining my network is that, with a number of projects in the feasibility or planning stages at any one time, we can connect you with the development that's ideal for your level of experience. We've been through all the steps of the ETHICAL framework many times, and we've built a network of developers, architects, engineers, builders and all the other people and teams involved in high impact property investments. These are teams and people we know you can trust and whose experience is a matter of record.

We can pair you with the project and the development team that will maximise your learning and minimise the stress of being involved in a bigger property project than you've likely ever worked on before.

It makes sense, and it beats taking the risk of going it alone and re-inventing the wheel. We have a wheel ready and waiting for you. And that's the end of our plug. Let's get back to you and the reality that is waiting for you.

Things to look out for and the pressure of going it alone.

When you're new to the business of property investment of this nature, it's almost impossible to make informed decisions. Your prior experience won't stand you in good stead when the scale of the project is so much bigger and more complex than anything you've done before.

Working in this space, there are so many more considerations than are involved in building a home and selling it. There are design requirements, specialist materials and sustainability considerations, permits to be sought and granted, and financial complexities that you probably haven't encountered in your previous investments.

Then again, negative emotions like fear and greed get in the way, and you can easily be misled. People you thought were your partners can quickly become people you'd rather not deal with, or worse, people you need to chase for even the simplest things like updates.

Let me tell you a story about Carrie, who wanted to get into investing.

Carrie attended a number of property networking events, and she saw that property was a great way to get the financial outcome that she wanted. She didn't have the time to do it herself, so she found a joint venture partner to work with.

The joint venture partner claimed to have the time and the skills to do the project and Carrie, through a combination of enthusiasm and FOMO, was eager to invest. In her haste, Carrie didn't bother with background research into the deal or the lady with whom she was joint venturing.

A number of months went by, and Carrie heard nothing. She didn't know what was happening and the date for the project to close was looming, yet she hadn't had any clear communication from the joint venture partner. When they spoke, she didn't really get the information or the answers that she wanted.

Eventually, reluctantly, Carrie got her lawyers involved. It turned out that the joint venture partner had sold the property they'd been planning to develop without informing Carrie. After a lot of unnecessary drama, expense and lost time, the joint venture partner ended up having to sell her own property to be able to pay Carrie back, and it was all very messy and difficult for everyone.

Carrie eventually got her money back with all the interest that was due, but it was a very stressful period of her life. And so the lessons learned emphasised the importance of:

- *completing detailed background research into the project*
- *understanding the terms of the deal and the people involved, and not take things on face value*

- *communicating regularly and effectively. It's essential that everyone in an active role in the investment needs to understand the importance of communicating in detail*

- *adhering to an agreed schedule of communications, set up at the beginning of the project.*

When things like what happened to Carrie occur, the ultimate downside is that you can lose money and then do not or cannot invest again. But it's not just the money that you've lost, it's the opportunity cost of what could have been realised for the people who would have benefited from the project — the residents as well as the investors.

When you invest in high impact projects, you're participating in something that's bigger than making money — it has the potential to make a massive impact on a lot of peoples' lives and create a success that will reverberate across our whole society.

That's why experience in the field, and a solid understanding of the processes and the people involved is so crucially important.

We're not just talking about your experience.

When we talk about experience, which may be something you have yet to gain, we're also talking about the experience your partners in whatever venture(s) you choose, can bring to the table. It is critical, especially in the period before you can consider yourself a seasoned veteran of ethical property investing, that anyone you go into business with has a high level of experience.

Ideally, your partners, whether you choose to amass a team yourself or join an established, credentialled syndicate, will have the analytical, planning, building, management and financial experience to turn an idea into a successful project. And that just happens to be a neat segue into the next chapter, in which we examine the value of your potential partners' track record.

For a special video relating to experience visit:

https://www.hipi.global/book/experience

SCAN ME

Chapter 5

T is for Track Record.

There's a fundamental difference between words and deeds which align to the fundamental difference between marketing materials and positive impacts and outcomes. People hear what you say, but they'll remember what you do.

In this chapter, we're going to be looking at your intentions versus your investment performance to date. We are also going to weigh the objectives, claims and evidence regarding social and environmental impact of the people you may be considering working with in property investment. In other words, their track record. And that doesn't necessarily refer to whether they did what they said they'd do, rather, it focuses on what impacts they've actually made in the past.

So, before we start we'll talk about what you should be looking for in the realm of social and environmental impact and responsibility. Perhaps more importantly, we'll give you some practical tips to use in assessing the claims and marketing material of developers and others you may be considering working with.

Beware of false labels.

When you go to the supermarket you can easily buy eggs that are labelled "natural" and "fresh" without knowing that the hens that laid the eggs are still caged and are enduring a crowded, dirty, difficult life. You can buy eggs that are labelled "free range", but that too can be a marketing ploy — in some "free range" facilities the roof opens so they can see the sky, but the hens are still locked inside.

But if you get eggs where the label explicitly tells you the indoor and/or outdoor densities of the hens onsite or bears proof that the producers meet RSPCA Approved or Humane Choice True Free Range standards, which are among the best for animal welfare[13], you are getting a measured, quantifiable benefit.

The point here being, beware of ploys, exaggerations, glib promises and outright fabrication when it comes to proposals for investing in allegedly ethical investments. The only way you can know for sure is to thoroughly check the track record of everyone involved. It's hard work and it takes time, but it's worth it.

A cautionary tale of two definitions: what does affordable *really* mean?

There are companies that use the NSW environmental planning system to provide "affordable housing". By using these government guidelines and working with community housing providers to ensure that a proportion of the stock is rented at 80% of market value, the developers qualify for a greater density on site, and consequently they receive more sales and/or rental income.

Let's stop here for a moment and examine what is really happening. From the developers' point of view, they are absolutely doing everything by the book. Fine. Now because of factors like the rent reduction on the affordable housing, there are sometimes complicating factors such as carpark allocation — do the spaces go to those paying full market value while some of the other tenants use street parking? An additional consideration is the impact on residents surrounding the development. The implications of the over-flow car parking on the streets, and the reduction of safety due to increased traffic movements, is often a trigger for community action against the developer.

However, the bigger issue is that having potentially spent years and years on the public housing register, those in need are still finding that 80% of the inflated housing market is still well beyond their reach. Particularly when the prices are sometimes influenced by those that can afford to pay more such as the double-income-with-no kids market or DINKS. When the demand for the homes drives up the price, the 80% of market value proposition becomes a bridge too far for other members of the community. For many single mothers, women over 55 or anybody on less than 2 incomes — this is definitely NOT affordable.

From a community standpoint, it may appear that the law allows developers to market the property as "affordable", which helps them achieve their income aims, however the social dividend is missing altogether. The company is meeting the standard, but the social benefit of building (truly) affordable homes for the people we are trying to help, that they can actually buy or rent… is missing. Now, the solution may be to involve community housing providers in the process right from the beginning to achieve a balance between addressing community needs, developers' commercial objectives and governmental oversight. Well, it would be a start.

Nonetheless, imagine you're an investor in a project such as this. In the end, the community backlash may tarnish the good you were hoping your investment would cultivate. And that can be a bit soul-destroying. So you really must scrutinise the plans, proposed outcomes and community benefit carefully, before getting involved in an ethical property investment syndicate.

Talking the talk v walking the walk.

As I've said before, the world is changing. There's a growing consciousness that the solutions to a great many of the world's problems lay within the hands of ordinary people like you and me. If everyone is making whatever difference they can, however small, it all adds up to a great deal of positive change.

And because we consumers have so much clout with the companies we do business with, a lot of companies, and even global corporations, are cottoning onto the fact that supporting positive change doesn't cost them money, it helps them generate more profits — along with a more motivated workforce, impressed and perhaps positively influenced suppliers, and happier shareholders.

The movement to business for good.

Around the world, more and more companies are choosing to commit to the UN Global Sustainable Development Goals — 17 different goals[14] with associated targets, actions, events and publications, that aim to enhance global sustainability. The goals range from ending poverty and hunger, to improving education, increasing equality and reducing inequality, to sustainable cities and communities, and responsible production and consumption.

When companies align with the UN Global Sustainable Development Goals, they measure and report their progress across each of the goals, and they're open about their results.

Similarly, a lot of businesses are now signing up to become B Corporations — businesses that will "make decisions to create a positive impact for their workers, customers, suppliers, community, and the environment"[15]. To qualify to market themselves as B Corps, these businesses are certified by an external party that assesses their impact on the community, the environment, and their workers and customers, and evaluates their governance using criteria such as ethics, transparency, accountability, and their social and environmental mission.

When you deal with an organisation that has committed to

the UN Goals, or is certified as a B Corp, you know that you're getting what's on the label. You know they use approved metrics to monitor, measure and report their impacts, so you can trust their intentions and communications.

Let's talk about just one high impact company.

Of course, not every firm that's committed to positive social and environmental impact is a B Corp or openly aligned to the UN's Global Sustainable Development Goals. Take one of the firms we've worked with and admire, Gensler.

A global architectural firm, Gensler has publicly committed to achieving net zero carbon dioxide emissions by 2030. Their website includes separate pages that detail their goals and actions in the areas of sustainability, diversity and community. They offer a wide range of key metrics to support their claims, including having completed over 700 US Green Building Council (GBC) certified projects. Their designs are energy and water efficient, and globally they claim to have saved 64 million tonnes of carbon dioxide emissions with resilient design strategies[16].

Just by reading their website you get a sense of their commitment — and you can always request supporting literature for every claim and promise they make. This is the kind of company we seek, investigate and ultimately, when we're satisfied that they really do walk the walk, work with.

It's worth the effort.

It's easy to fall into the trap of believing a developer when they talk the talk about affordable housing, sustainability or building resilient communities. But before you commit your money to a project, you need to see the evidence that it will be what it purports or aspires to be, backed by a track record of similar successes.

The good news is, when you find a team that has consistently delivered on their promises, they'll be happy to share the metrics of their impact with you, and that will build your confidence. Because when they get it right, the impact can be enormously beneficial and widespread.

When you do find a group or organisation that exhibits behaviours and can demonstrate a track record that are commensurate with your values and goals (see Chapter 09 — A is for Aligned Values) you have an opportunity to create the legacy you want in good conscience and assurance.

So! How to assess a developer's track record?

We've already talked about why you need to assess the developer's history before you commit your money to a project they'll be in charge of realising. Just to recap, it's about figuring out whether their promises are genuine, and whether they've delivered on their promises over previous projects.

It's all about peace of mind, and having the confidence that your objectives — financial, social and environmental — will be obtained.

But there's more to it than that. If you choose the right developer or development team, you'll get the benefit of leveraging from their experience. A true professional will give you access to better quality projects, because they have a depth of understanding about the complex logistics and organisational demands of the process.

If a development team has a breadth and length of experience, they'll understand the market and will be responsive to the opportunities and threats each turn of the property cycle presents.

The longer a developer has been in business, the more likely it is that they've been through some tough times, so they'll be more risk aware, and more capable of dealing with the unforeseen.

A "newbie" — especially one who's started out in order to take advantage of the boom part of the cycle — is more likely to believe that, as there's a boom going on, nothing serious can go wrong.

Booms, busts, and getting burnt...a property cycle primer.

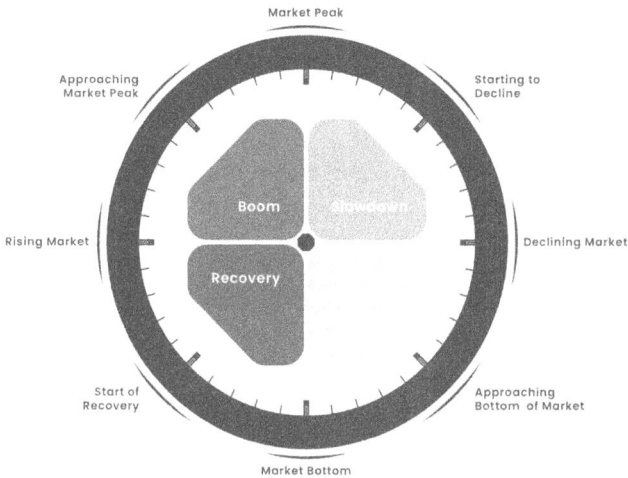

Market Peak

Approaching
Market Peak

Starting to
Decline

Rising Market

Boom

Slowdown

Recovery

Declining Market

Start of
Recovery

Approaching
Bottom of Market

Market Bottom

5. The Property Cycle

Having introduced the concept of the property cycle in that last paragraph and mentioned one of the two associated 'B' words (the other one is bust), it occurs to me that I should have a short discussion of these concepts, just so we're all on the same page.

In a nutshell, the property cycle is a recognised progression that obeys no schedules, and often defies logic, as it moves through four distinct phases:

1. **The boom.**

   This is the one that gets everyone excited. Prices are climbing, market activity is frenetic and decision-making is often highly emotional rather than rational, and dollar signs appear in everybody's eyes. People who

*have never been in the property market before find their
way in, and the madness reaches a whole new level. But
remember these 4 truths:*

✓ Building your investment property at the right
time in the boom is a passport to exciting returns.

✓ Buying or building in a boom that's just about to
go bust can leave you high and dry.

✓ Selling in a boom market can be a moment of glory.

✓ For investors, speed is of the essence, because
booms can be notoriously short-lived.

2. *The downturn.*

*As the market becomes more chaotic and prices get
too crazy, the whole thing overheats, supply begins to
outweigh demand and demand itself starts tapering off.
All those developers who were late to the party during
the boom are left with empty properties and soaring
debt. Vacancy levels rise, panic selling begins, and prices
slide even further. Those with effective escape plans/exit
strategies activate them — preferably sooner rather
than later.*

3. *Stabilisation.*

*When the supply and demand curves drift back towards
each other and the fear and alarm give way to more
rational thinking, prices stabilise and people begin to
take stock. While buyers are creeping back into the
market, there's still enough stock to keep prices fairly*

flat. Developers remain gun shy, but for the few that recognise which stage the cycle has reached, opportunities abound.

4. **The upturn.**

   Once the progression has reached its lowest point, commonly referred to as the bottom of the cycle, the only way is up, and that's the way it goes. Vacancy rates fall, rents get back to a more normal level, and returns to investors become more attractive. As demand grows and supply lags, thanks to developer lethargy in the often-lengthy stabilisation period, prices begin to rise. As the market gathers pace, the return to boom conditions becomes inevitable.

This matters because it helps you objectively assess track records.

The cyclical nature of the property industry is an accepted fact of life, but it's incredibly hard to read it accurately. There are ghost signals from the market, "black swan" events that can spin the wheel backwards or forwards in a moment, local variations and a whole range of other pitfalls.

If the developer you're considering working with has been around for a long time, they've almost certainly been through a number of cycles, and have therefore more than likely learned to read the signs better than most. If they've been through one or more particularly brutal cycles — say if they were around in the GFC of 2008 — and they're still in business, that's a good indicator that they are smart operators.

To have survived numerous property cycles, let alone thrived throughout, shows you that they've probably developed sharp analytical skills and creative problem-solving abilities.

It also indicates that they've most likely assembled a reliable team, one that they've been able to keep together through the good times and the bad. That's another sign of trustworthiness.

It's question time and here are the 6 questions you need to ask.

To put it plainly, when it comes time to assess the merits of developers who can handle your high impact property investment, you need to ask relevant, pointed questions. The answers you get should shape your decision, because they'll give you a clear indication of the experience and track record of the developers you're vetting.

I shouldn't have to add, but I will, that if the developer you're talking to gets annoyed, evasive or secretive about their past, that's a red flag. The right developer will always be open about their past, their processes and their track record.

So, to the questions:

1. *How long have you been in business?*

    This is a relatively easy one, but the answer is telling. It allows you to work out how many property cycles the business has been through (there's a graph that will help you on the Business Insider website[17]). Of course, the longer they've survived, the better.

2. *How many property developments have you completed?*

   Again, a fairly easily answered question, and the answer is simple but illustrative — as long as you follow up with some supplementary questions:

   a. *What is the average value of your developments?*

   b. *What is the cumulative value of your developments?*

   c. *What is the average return to investors?*

   d. *Have you had any developments go bad?*

3. *How long has your current team been together?*

   This is an interesting one. A less trustworthy developer may have been through a number of architect/builder/ financier/business teams before, burning people and then moving on. That's not necessarily the case if the team hasn't been together long, but it is a signal that you need to ask more questions.

4. *What is your experience in high impact property developments?*

   Ask them to describe the projects to you, how were they conceived and what the outcomes were, including the crucial follow-up:

   a. *Can you provide impact metrics around the social, environmental and financial benefits of your projects?*

5. *What is your investor management process?*

    b. *Do you have a regular communications schedule?*

    c. *Are you available to answer investor questions throughout the process?*

6. *Can you provide testimonials and introduce me to some of your investors?*

It is essential that you check references for anyone you intend to work with, even if you're convinced that they are the right development team for you. Check their testimonials and if possible, talk to previous or current investors to ensure that they've come good on promises on prior projects.

As exhausting as this may have been, it isn't an exhaustive list and I'm sure you can come up with more yourself, but the point is, it's important to ask questions so you can gauge the developer's track record. The developer's attitude to the questions, and the depth of their answers, will give you a good idea of their communications skills and their willingness to be transparent and accountable, too.

Meet a good developer.

I've known Symon Peters of the 360 Collective for some years.

Born in New Zealand, Symon grew up on a farm, and it taught him to be a hard worker. Turning to property development when he was just in his 20s, Symon worked on a number of high-profile projects, including a 200 unit apartment building. Importantly, in that development he worked with council to include affordable housing. He was also the first in New Zealand to buy airspace over a Council owned Car park to build taller buildings and utilise extra airspace in Auckland City.

After moving to Australia, Symon's first project acquisition was a very large hotel development in Cairns. It was by no means his last. Having now amassed almost 35 years in property development, Symon has facilitated the development of over $500 million worth of properties.

In 2019 Symon set up the 360 Collective, a specialist development advisory firm. In addition to managing its own projects, the Collective helps other developers fill the gaps in their development teams. Somehow, Symon also finds the time to mentor aspiring property developers and investors, and he has been one of my greatest inspirations and educators.

Before I did any business with Symon I checked out his credentials, delved into his track record, and examined his experience in the kind of developments in which I was interested. It wasn't a fluke that we met, just good, solid detective work on my part. I can introduce you to other developers of Symon's calibre, or you can use the questions and process outlined above to find your own. It's entirely your choice. Either way, the general advice applies: do your research… please!

Your turn — let's talk about your track record.

> *Becoming a high impact property investor is a journey, and like any journey, to figure out how to get where you're going, you need to know the starting point. That's why it's essential that you interrogate and understand your own track record in the property arena.*

When investors come on board with the High Impact Property Investment Network, we always help them audit their own investment history by:

- ✦ *investigating whether their profits have been what they hoped and expected*

- ✦ *asking about the social, environmental, sustainability and community resilience aspects of their previous projects*

- ✦ *encouraging them to consider their future intent on those issues, and whether that intent could or should be modified*

In any case, they need to be honest about whether or not their intent was realised.

I strongly recommend that you conduct a similar self-audit. Although it helps to have an independent observer walk through this with you, it is something you can do yourself if you're unflinchingly honest and prepared for the answers you receive.

Negative vs positive gearing.

I'm going to go out on a limb here and guess that if you have property investments, you're either using them as a tax deduction through negative gearing, or you think that negative gearing is a good idea and you're keen to try it.

Actually, that's not really going out on a limb because in 2019, of over 2.2 million Australians who owned one or more investment properties, over 58% made a net loss on those properties. Those investors claimed the losses against tax and were thereby classed as negatively geared investors[18].

If you're one of those people, I wish you luck and I don't want to sound too harsh, but I think you're doing it wrong.

Here's why we don't endorse negative gearing.

When you negatively gear your property, you're betting that the capital gain you make when you sell it at some time in the future will outweigh the losses you make on it year in and year out. Yes, you will be claiming tax deductions on those losses, which will make up for some of the money you sink into the property, but at the end of the day (or at least the end of the tax year), you still have less money in your pocket.

We all know people who have a great negative gearing story. You know — "I bought the property for $350,000 and sold it ten years later for $500,000, so I made $150k". That's fine, except it doesn't take into account ten years of interest, property management fees, repairs and maintenance and other costs paid out of their own pocket for all those years. Not to mention the capital gains tax on the sale figure.

The truth is, even with tax deductions, you're losing cash in hand every year, and there's no guarantee that the profit you make when you sell will even cover those costs, let alone leave you with extra cash.

The proof is in the pudding.

Okay, let's do some work with numbers to better illustrate what I have been talking about. We are going to do a very simplified exercise, based on the tax calculator at moneysmart.gov.au and using the 2021/22 tax year.

If your income is $120,000 for that year, the tax you pay is $29,467. If you claim $2000 a month in losses against your investment property (that's $2000 a month in outgoings you have to find), your taxable income becomes $96,000 and you pay $21,667 in tax. In other words, of the $24,000 you paid out, $7,800 is returned to you.

Your actual cost is still $16,200 per annum. Extrapolate that across ten years, and you're $162,000 in the hole. Using the "$150,000" profit mentioned above, your actual loss is $12,000 ($350,000 purchase price + $162,000 lost costs = $512,000).

There are a few other issues with negative gearing, too. If you're relying on negative gearing, rising interest rates, higher vacancy rates and other unforeseen events can hit you harder. It also limits the number of properties you can buy, because your disposable income is being reduced by the amount of losses not covered by your tax deductions, and that restricts the amount of money you can borrow.

And that's why we don't "do" negative gearing. I am not saying that the above scenario will be the case for everyone, and you may think you're earning so much money you really need to take a loss, but for most of us, positively geared makes so much more sense.

The simple joy of positive gearing.

Here's how positive cash flow works. You buy a property with a loan and the income is higher than the costs/expenses. So after tax you have money in your pocket. This is the model we recommend. Yes, you pay tax on those earnings, but wouldn't you rather have extra money left over at the end of the month than be in the red.

Using the same tax calculator we used above, let's do the sums. Let's say that instead of taking a $2000 loss each month, you make a modest $1000 on your investment property. Your income goes from $120,000 to $132,000. You'll pay an additional $4,400 in tax, so of your $12,000 in income you retain $7,600. Over ten years, that's a handy $76,000.

Some people will claim that positively geared properties are only available in areas where rental income is flat and capital growth is slow. I'm not so sure about that, because a rising tide floats all boats, but unless the value of your positively geared property is actually going backwards, you'll still be in front.

What this all means for you.

Now, that was a lengthy diversion to help you make an honest appraisal of your track record thus far, in case you've fallen for the hype around negative gearing. Do the sums and see how it's worked for you. You may be unpleasantly surprised (of course you may not be, and if so, well done).

If you are disappointed at your bottom line thus far, it just illustrates my point that not knowing how your investments are truly performing means you're just stabbing in the dark. It's confusing because you don't know where you're starting. If you are negative gearing, you are probably going backwards, so it's not sustainable. You can end up realising that you do not have enough for retirement, and that's stressful.

When you're not sleeping at night because you have all these properties draining you, it's not fun. Remember, more sustainable cash flow means more money in your pocket. This means you have a higher income, so you have a higher borrowing capacity, so you're able to make more of an impact.

And that's track records.

To sum up the gist of this chapter, you really need to understand a development team's history and have evidence of their positive impacts before you commit any money to a project. I think I have given you enough leads and questions to ask to help you along there.

But it's equally important that you understand your own track record, and if needs be, modify your investment strategy and expectations. I know there's a lot to take in, but the rewards will come, I can assure you. And if you need help, I can match you with developers and teams that consistently deliver successful outcomes.

So your next task will be to consider what kind of outcomes you desire — and you'll find some guidance on that in the next chapter.

For a special video relating to track record visit:
https://www.hipi.global/book/trackrecord

Chapter 6

H is for high impact.

Houses that are built to inspire, create and establish positive impacts are what we like to call "homes" because that is where our heart has always been.

Back in the introductory chapter, I wrote about Maslow's hierarchy of needs, but I want to go back to it for a moment to emphasise just how critical where and how you live can be to so many of the layers of that hierarchy. Beyond meeting the need for shelter and a place to eat, sleep and stay secure, your home can be a source of the love and belonging, and the self-esteem, that Maslow posited were essential milestones on the path to self-actualisation.

A home that combines comfort and personal safety with a feeling of belonging, a wider communal sense of security, and the pride of knowing that your home is making a positive contribution to the future of the planet, is a home that you can't help but love.

That's what High Impact Property Investments is all about. We strongly believe that by building affordable homes that are also sustainable and help to create resilient communities, we're making it possible for our residents to meet their potential and to make a positive impact on our society.

Why we want to turn a steady trickle of high impact property investing into a mainstream movement

In a world of rising prices and falling real wages, mounting waste and pollution, depleting resources and climate change linked to the burning of fossil fuels, the need for affordable, sustainable living is growing faster than ever.

Yet a lot of people probably haven't heard or know much about terms like affordable housing, building resilient communities, or Specialised Disability Accommodation (SDA). Almost everybody would by now have a clear understanding of sustainability, but probably assume that in terms of housing, it's too expensive, or because they already own a home, it doesn't apply to them.

We need to change the lack of knowledge about affordability, resilience and sustainability because:

✦ *Real wages have been falling in Australia since the second half of 2020[19], and over half of low-income families renting homes in Australia, suffer from "housing stress", in which over 30% of the household income is spent on housing costs (rent, rates, water and power etc)[20].*

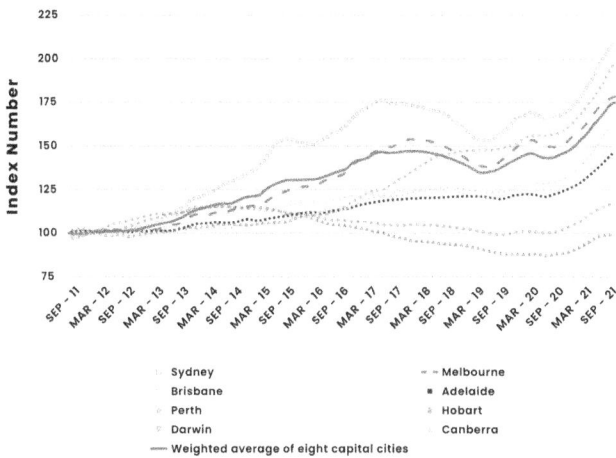

Legend:
- Sydney
- Brisbane
- Perth
- Darwin
- – – Melbourne
- Adelaide
- Hobart
- Canberra
- —— Weighted average of eight capital cities

6. Residential Property Price Indexes Across
8 Australian Capital Cities

✦ *Mass migration from capital cities to regional areas, espe-cially along the eastern seaboard has become increasingly commonplace. This has happened, in part, because since the pandemic that has changed all our lives swept onto the scene, we discovered that not only could a lot of us work from home, "home" could be anywhere.*

✦ *Rising costs keep rising because demand has outstripped supply, interest rates remain low, and government grants designed to help first home buyers get into the market have only exacerbated rising prices. In the September quarter of 2021 alone, the weighted average of property prices across Australia's eight capital cities rose by 5.0% for the quarter, making the average rise over the previous 12 months a staggering 21.7%[21].*

✦ *It's getting harder and harder to buy or to rent, particularly for lower income earners. Fifty people inspecting a rental property is not uncommon, and although the rent has usually already been put up because of the demand, keen candidates are bidding higher. Some (say they've just sold their city home and are cashed up) will not only "gazump" other potential renters, they'll stump up 12 months' rent in advance. For people on the lower end of the economic scale, it's impossible to compete.*

For our society to remain a stable, secure and cohesive community, we need to address the housing issues that are beginning to undermine the values we all wish to live by.

Let's look at each of the aspects of high impact property investment and consider the need, the opportunities for investors and the benefits to the stakeholders and the wider community.

Affordable housing is so ~~important~~ critical!

The simple definition of affordable housing is that which costs 30% or less of household income, including rent or mortgage, council rates, electricity, gas and water. As housing prices rose, the pandemic caused job losses and underemployment (people working fewer hours than they would prefer or working in jobs for which they are overqualified just to make ends meet), and many Australians have been pushed into the low or very low-income earner bracket.

For people in that situation, finding any housing is getting ever more difficult and often if they have to commit to a home that consumes a high percentage of their income, they fall into housing stress. The wait for government-supplied social housing can be up to 10 years, which is so long almost anything could happen.

There is a huge amount of pent-up demand for affordable housing. And as I have already shown in earlier chapters, for investors and developers who approach the task the right way, building affordable housing can bear excellent returns.

The costs to society are lower when housing is affordable.

When society as a whole benefits, we all win and the perceived costs become a fast-disappearing speck in the rear view mirror as people's lives are positively impacted.

People who can comfortably afford their homes:

✓ feel secure in them and become part of the local community

✓ are much less likely to be disruptive or to incur costs on society

✓ enjoy improved health

✓ are less likely to commit or become victims of crime

✓ are better placed to contribute to the good of the community

✓ find their need for social services including health care, the justice system and addiction services, falls[22].

The impact of providing affordable housing has a multiplier affect across the entire community. And the fact that you can earn double digit returns while investing in it, means there's no reason not to do it. As long as you do it right.

Amy's story.

Amy Degenhart from DegenhartShedd; a colleague of mine, a developer and architect, was interested in creating an afford-able housing project in Southport, on the Gold Coast. Amy went to the Director of Planning of the Gold Coast City Council, and put in a case for a small lot housing project built in a high-rise zone but designed and constructed it as low rise at the same (high rise) density. This was more appealing to the community. Among the advantages of building low rise was the fact that the costs would be much lower.

There were quite a lot of issues to overcome, but Amy persisted and created ten small lot subdivision dwellings. She sold the units "off the plan" as house and land packages, so the buyers could contribute to the design and fitout of their own small lot home.

The neighbours were very supportive because they could see what she was trying to do, but Amy faced hesitancy from first home buyers unsure of whether the project was appropriate for them. Eventually seven of the ten units were bought by first home buyers, and the result has been the creation of a genuinely-affordable, little living community.

These people need affordable housing?

As you might expect, low and moderate-income earners are the targets for affordable housing.

It's a struggle for young professionals on early-career wages to get into the housing market and affordable homes are the solution they need.

However, the greatest need is often among single women, especially those over 55 or those with children. For far too many women who are unable to work long or regular hours because of their parenting responsibilities, or women who've been out of the workforce for lengthy periods, the only housing solutions available include couch surfing or living in cars.

There are a number of factors that make it harder for women:

1. *The gender pay gap and subsequent lower superannuation accumulation.*

2. *Taking time out of the workforce to have and look after children.*

3. *Australia has a 38% divorce rate[23] and unfortunately it is most often the women that fare worse financially in the aftermath, which can lead to difficulties in securing affordable accommodation.*

There are a multitude of negative consequences of being unable to find affordable housing, needing to live in cars or imposing on friends and relatives, and having no fixed address at which to receive official correspondence. These can range from an inability to find employment, to lack of self-esteem and dignity for women and low-income earners. As I mentioned above, the costs of such "solutions" often rebounds onto society, so the benefits of funding affordable housing are most certainly high impact.

The good news... (please, at last).

According to the Australian government, some 1 million social and affordable homes will be required to meet community requirements by 2036[24]. That means that not only is the need recognised and quantified, the federal and state governments will be motivated to assist in meeting that need. There's a boom in affordable housing design and construction coming. The question is, will you be part of it?

Sustainable homes are, of course, the answer.

Sustainable housing is a concept most of us are familiar with, and I would guess approve of. A sustainable home or building is one that is energy efficient and made with components and materials designed to minimise waste and create a non-toxic environment for human health.

Why we need to embrace sustainability.

The business of constructing, running and maintaining homes and buildings is responsible for around 25% of Australia's greenhouse gas emissions[25]. Manufacturing building components, from concrete and steel reinforcement to bricks, tiles, floorcoverings, plumbing and electrical cabling and appliances, uses a lot of energy and consumes a lot of fossil fuels, causing greenhouse gas emissions. Further emissions are generated in transporting materials. The building process also produces a lot of waste, a great deal of which goes to landfill. In addition, the process can employ toxic materials that can exude gases that are harmful to human health.

Once completed, artificially heating and cooling homes and buildings uses a lot of energy. This contributes to our rising greenhouse gas emissions and subsequent accumulation in the atmosphere, which has an effect on the environment.

To extend the life of buildings and homes, you need to be constantly maintaining and repairing them, and every so often you'll need to renovate to keep the place liveable. But even a few years extra between renovations can save a lot of money, a lot of waste and a significant volume of greenhouse gases.

It's not as difficult as it sounds.

Creating durable, sustainable dwellings and businesses is about smart design, careful materials and fitout selection, and healthy common sense.

Contributing factors to sustainability can be as simple as orienting the structure to take advantage of winter sunshine and maximise natural cooling in summer (i.e., in Australia, facing north), and implementing energy efficient materials and techniques in building. Including effective ceiling and wall insulation, and double-glazing windows, can reduce the need for artificial cooling and heating, and lower ongoing living costs.

For people like us, interested in making affordable homes, working with modular designs can reduce the waste generated in the manufacturing and building process, and the smaller the overall space, the cheaper a home is to run. Minimising the use of toxic materials is a no-brainer on a number of levels. And installing energy efficient appliances can further contribute to lower living costs.

Further augmenting sustainability through measures like solar energy and batteries, rainwater tanks and grey water recycling, will increase the value and lower the environmental impact of the dwelling. Of course, these will require some additional investment at the outset, but will repay you as time progresses. Given that from 2009 — 2019 electricity prices rose 100% and water and sewerage costs rose 66% in Australia[26], you would expect that the dividends from investing in energy and water efficiency will only continue to grow.

Here's a short checklist.

So, in short, here are just half a dozen ways you can make the dwellings you invest in (including your own) more sustainable:

1. *Pay attention to the orientation.*

2. *Make the most of passive heating and cooling.*

3. *Don't use toxic materials.*

4. *Don't build any bigger than is necessary.*

5. *Use energy efficient appliances.*

6. *Consider solar energy and batteries, rainwater tanks and grey water recycling.*

When you incorporate these simple principles into your building program —

✓ the home is more comfortable

✓ the environment is better for your health

✓ space is used more efficiently

And even if the initial cost is a little higher, in the long run it will cost less overall.

The benefits of sustainability are there for all to see

Imagine the rewards of knowing that the people who live in the homes you build are able to divert the money they would previously have expended on energy and associated living costs, to things that allow them to thrive and grow. And at the same time, slow the emission of greenhouse gases into our atmosphere.

According to the IPCC we are responsible for climate change and we have ten years to turn the ship around. So the ultimate upside of embracing sustainability is that we can ensure a future for ourselves or our children.

A personal note on sustainability.

It's beyond the scope of this book, but I wanted to share with you some ideas on making your own lifestyle more sustainable. This isn't a lecture, just a guide.

There are some great resources available on how to make a home more sustainable, and Yourhome.gov.au is a fabulous place to start. It shows you the key areas to focus on and gives you ideas on improving your carbon footprint, no matter what kind of home you live in.

And if you think that because your home is well established you can't do much to help (or your high impact investment is based on existing structures) consider this — there's a growing industry of home renovation professionals who can retrofit any dwelling to improve its sustainability.

Kahkoon Technologies LLC is one company we work with in this area. They have developed a net zero home prototype, in which they winterise the homes by insulating the walls and roof, and use double glazed windows. They also install smart technology that can diagnose problems such as burst or leaking pipes before they become big, costly problems and put in solar panels and batteries in for energy efficiency.

Building resilient communities.

Well-rounded, interactive communities don't just happen by accident, they are built by design with the future and future generations in mind.

Resilient communities are places where all the residents are connected and enjoy the feeling of cohesion that comes with living there. They share resources, look out for each other, work side by side in community gardens, and support each other.

Resilient communities recover much more quickly and effectively when adversity strikes — a crucial quality in a world where we are beset by extreme weather events like floods, drought and cyclones, economic disasters, and physical catastrophes like earthquakes, fires and pandemics. When these things strike, resilient communities bring out the best in people.

A lot of the housing estates I see advertised these days are more insular than social in their design. The block sizes may be getting smaller, but we're becoming less inclined to get outside and explore the neighbourhood. The kids are glued to their devices and playing video games and the adults drive in and drive out, often never even seeing their neighbours, let alone saying "g'day".

We're building a world in which there's less and less human connection, and it will only get worse unless we consciously design for it. We need to recognise what makes a resilient community and strive to make each development we create an example of what can be achieved when we design for it.

Introducing The Triangle.

Before I became a property developer, I saw something on tv that really inspired and motivated me. Kevin McCloud, the host of an addictive ABC program called "Grand Designs" visits people and talks about the design and construction of their homes, and their renovations. He devoted two episodes, however, to a development he put together called The Triangle, in Swindon, England.

This "grand" endeavour at creating a small, diverse community of sustainable and affordable homes, features a wonderful array of innovations in design and construction. The external walls are made out of hempcrete — a material based on the hemp plant that sequesters more carbon dioxide than is used in creating it. The central open spaces are designed to soak up rainwater, to avoid flooding, ensure the gardens remain lush and green, and ensure less water simply goes down the drain. Every home is connected with the others via a "shimmy", a kind of electronic tablet that allows them to communicate, and share news and ideas. And the whole thing is built around a communal space with community gardens and meeting/ interactive places that encourage the spirit of togetherness.

There's much more that's fascinating and ground-breaking about the design, but the sales and rental arrangement are equally innovative. There's a wonderful mix of "social rented" dwellings for lower income residents, "intermediate rented" units in which residents pay 80% of market rent, and "rent to buy" units in which the residents rent at low prices to allow them to save for a deposit to eventually buy the place.

To me, The Triangle[27] is a sterling example of what it means to build a resilient community, and something I'd love to replicate.

Specialist Disability Accommodation — the good news and the even better news

Creating specialist disability accommodation is necessarily a specialised undertaking that requires a different approach to design, construction and management. SDA dwellings are built for people living with extreme functional impairments or particularly high care needs, who meet the specialist disability accommodation funding requirements.

The home must be specially designed and may include features such as reinforced ceilings to allow for the instal-lation of hoists, and other assistive technology. It needs to meet the criteria for classification within one of five design categories, ranging from "basic" to "high physical support", and be an apartment, a villa, duplex or townhouse, or free-standing house. SDA providers need to enrol the dwelling in the scheme, and if successful, accommodation will be funded by the National Disability Insurance Scheme (NDIS).

The good news is that with funding for SDA at approximately $700 million per annum[28], and new builds providing some 52% of the growth in SDA stock[29], the availability of developer, design and construction expertise required is clearly growing.

I'm sure I don't need to detail the impact that having access to Specialist Disability Accommodation would have on the lives of the people who would benefit from your investment in SDA. Imagine the sense of independence, security and potential that a person living with disability would feel on moving in.

Make an impact.

This book is an interesting mix of hard fact and beautiful feelings. You can make money by investing in property the traditional way, without considering such details as the affordability or sustainability of the dwellings you create, or the resilience of the communities you build.

But why would you?

In this chapter I have shown you, in my modest way, the massive and durable impact you can make on the lives of people who most need it. Elsewhere, I've already informed you of the kind of returns you can expect to earn from such investments — historically in the double digits for all of my high impact property investments so far.

But the one thing I can't show or tell you about is the personal reward you get from investing in high impact properties. It's something you have to experience yourself — and you will, every time you drive or walk past one of your developments. I urge you to experience it, just once. It's all about building a legacy, and this is one you can be proud of.

Of course, I would be remiss if I didn't provide you with information on the risks all investment types, including these, carry, and how to deal with them. So that's the topic of the next chapter — let's get into it while we're on a roll.

For a special video relating to high impact visit:
https://www.hipi.global/book/highimpact

Chapter 7

I is for Investment Risk.

Knowing yourself, know what you're willing to stand for and knowing what you won't abide is the beginning of what it means to understand, manage and mitigate risk.

As an investor, you are always taking on a certain amount of risk, no matter what you invest in. The price of shares can crash, the gold market could suddenly collapse and property investment carries a range of risks across every aspect of the process.

The carrot here is the financial rewards on offer for the investor, and it is a well-known truth in all forms of investing that the higher the risk, the higher the potential returns.

You can put your money on long term deposit at virtually no risk — the Australian Government guarantees bank deposits to $250,000 per account holder and per ADI (authorised deposit-taking institution — i.e. banks and credit societies)[30], but the returns at present can struggle to keep up with inflation.

At the other end of the scale, start-up companies and high-risk ventures like feature films can provide spectacular returns (who doesn't wish they'd invested in Crocodile Dundee back in 1986?), but the risk of losing it all is much higher than other investment options.

So before you go into high impact property investing — or any other investment for that matter — you need to understand the risks involved, and be prepared to wear the consequences. That means understanding your own appetite for risk. Be honest about whether you can afford to make the investment, and perhaps not see your money or any returns on it for some time, at least. And ask yourself seriously what would happen if the whole deal went south and you got nothing back.

Of course, there are measures you can take to reduce or modify the risk of any investment and the primary tool in your kit here is knowledge. The more you know about what you're planning to invest in, the more you'll grasp the nature and extent of the risks involved and the more confident you'll be about the outcome. The more you know about the people involved, about their track records, experience, attitudes, practices and processes, the more you can be assured that they know what they're doing and that they will deliver on their promises.

Once you have committed to an investment, the trick is not to just push the send button on the bank transfer and hope for the best. You need to be engaged in the progression towards a result, and to monitor the risks and changing conditions, so you don't get a rude shock at the end if things don't go exactly as planned.

This chapter is about understanding your own appetite for risk, the risks associated with property investment, and how to mitigate them. I've also included a section on transparency and accountability, because working with people who:

✓ communicate well and openly,

✓ answer questions,

✓ share difficult information early,

… can be a big factor in arming you with the knowledge that will help you accept and deal with the risks involved.

One more thing before we move on to a few paragraphs about knowing your own risk profile. You're reading this because you're keen on making money from high impact property investment, so I am assuming that you have at least a passing acquaintance with the risks that such an investment engenders.

So let's just think about another risk for a moment: the risk of not doing anything about sustainability, affordable housing, creating resilient communities or building specialist disability accommodation. If we continue to let marginalised people in the community become further marginalised, and don't at least attempt to stabilise our climate by being more sustainable, the risks (and costs) to us all will keep growing.

I can't guarantee that your venture in high impact property investing will be successful, even if I can show you a history of success measured in high returns. But I can guarantee you that one successful foray into this arena will have an impact on the lives of people you don't even know exist. And by giving those people the opportunity to reach their potential, you're creating the possibility that your legacy will be multiplied far beyond what you imagine.

Knowing your risk profile.

Before you even begin looking at possible ventures or properties in which you will invest, you need to know what your risk profile is. That is, you need to know what you expect of your investments, how much you are prepared to lose, and how much work you're prepared to do to protect your investment.

Beyond knowing your own risk profile, you also need to be prepared to back your knowledge with rational decision making. That is, when something comes along that is in conflict with your appetite for risk, but you feel emotionally compelled or externally pressured to invest anyway, you need to be able to make the tough decisions.

Meet John.

A professional worker with a high paying but non-permanent contract, John approached us to join one of our syndicate projects. John was no newbie, he had experience in syndicate investing and he understood the process well. He was excited about the opportunity to join our syndicate and about the possibility of earning excellent returns.

However, when it came to committing his funds, John kept stalling, making excuses and asking questions that we'd already answered before. Sensing that something wasn't quite right, I got in touch with John and probed a bit. It turned out that although he had the money and he was convinced that working with us would be a good investment, his personal risk profile had changed somewhat recently. For a start, he and his partner had been trying to conceive a baby, and although they had not yet been successful, he was hopeful that they soon would be. In addition, what with the pandemic and the global uncertainty that has been one of its results, he felt that his job was no longer as secure as it had been — there was no guarantee that his contract would be renewed.

It was an honest conversation that clarified for both of us where his risk profile was really at, and what the right answer was for him. He was conflicted because he wanted to have the success and the income that would come with the investment, but he wanted to do the best thing for his family. Taking on any risk at that time and in those circumstances — where his job might disappear or family circumstances may require him at home more, either of which would affect his cash position — just wasn't the right thing.

I was disappointed that we'd lost such a thoughtful investor, but I was sure John had done the right thing.

How to determine your risk profile.

When you're considering investing, it's important to know your risk profile because it helps you decide whether or not to go ahead, and it gives you the confidence to know that you've made the right decision. As I mentioned above, the greater the risk, the higher the potential rewards, but of course the greater the possibility that you could lose some or even all of your money. You have to feel comfortable with the fact that you could lose money.

So lesson one is simple: only invest what you can afford to lose.

Don't take your last ten dollars and put it on number 6 in race 4 at Randwick. Don't buy a lotto ticket because you need more for the rent than you have. Don't invest money that you can't afford to lose.

Invest because you're willing to or can afford to lose at least some of your money, if not all. It's a hard thing for me to say, because I know so many people who've done well out of high impact property investments, but I have to be realistic. That means facing the possibility that things can go wrong — things beyond anyone's control, or mistakes that you can't recover from can be made — and while such catastrophic losses are very rare in the property arena, they can happen.

What level of risk are you comfortable with?

What level of risk are you prepared to take with the funds you're willing to invest? Low, medium or high? Now, before you answer that, think about part 2 at the same time: what kind of returns do you want to earn — high, medium or low? The point being that you need to temper your expectations of return to the level of risk you're willing to accept. Find the balance that suits you, and work with it.

Think in terms of time.

In determining that balance, you should consider your age and how long you intend to invest for. Then again, if you're going to need to get your initial stake back within a shorter period, preferably with a juicy return (perhaps to buy a new home or fund an extended sabbatical to, let's say, write a book), maybe you decide to take a higher risk. It all depends on your present and future plans.

Are you already exposed?

Do you have other investments, and if so, what in? What sort of risk/return levels are they offering? Do you have any current or expected costs that will erode your ability to meet your commitments without the investment money? How is your track record in the investment sphere?

Stay at it until you get a result.

When you're trying to determine your risk profile, the internal struggle can be really intense, especially if you don't have a lot of experience in the area. The conflict between rationality and emotion can be hard to resolve. And there's always the underlying stress at the possibility of losing your whole investment.

But if you don't work on determining your risk profile and stick to the conclusions it demands, you can make some poor decisions which will ultimately lead to losses. Some people take on projects that don't match their risk profile, invest all their money into one project or let emotions like fear and greed get in the way of rational decision making. By taking the time and effort to investigate your investment risk profile and understand it, you'll take on projects that match your profile.

By working within your profile, you'll most likely include a buffer so that if there is a problem with an investment you're not wiped out. It's more sustainable, it helps you stay in the game longer, and it helps you sleep at night.

Minimising your risk — the key to better sleep.

Once you become clear on your risk profile, the next step is to gain a good handle on the risks inherent in property development and what you can do to minimise or mitigate them.

Being across the type of things that can go wrong should sharpen your enthusiasm for conducting due diligence on any property investment you're entertaining as a possibility. You'll know what to look for and how to look for it, be able to weigh up whether it's within your risk profile, and if needs be take steps to modify the risks you identify.

So what are the risks?

Some will be things to look out for, some are deal-breakers, and some are "black swan" events that you won't see coming. If the latter do occur, you'll be glad you listened to the advice about only investing what you can afford to lose. Once again, I must emphasise that such events are rare, but they do happen, and I would not be comfortable keeping that fact from you.

First, a deal-breaker.

Investing in property development is not a short-term speculation. Your money will be tied up for the medium to long term. In the case of high impact property investments, where you get in at the planning stage, any returns can be a year or more away. Approvals must be sought, designs finalised, earthworks and site preparations made, and the build and fitout itself completed. All that can take many months. Then, depending on whether you're going to sell or rent, it could still be weeks or months before you get any income.

It's not like the share market, where if things start to deteriorate you can simply sell your shares and get out — you're in it for the long haul and so is your money. If that lack of liquidity is not acceptable to you, the property investment market is not for you.

However, if you factor in the delays and are comfortably able to accommodate them, the returns can be well worth the wait.

Fundamental risks and how to mitigate them.

These are risks that are inherent to the business of property investing, but unlike the liquidity issue should not be deal-breakers. They can be significantly eased through methodical research, a thorough appreciation of the market conditions in the area of the development, and careful vetting of the people you'll be working with.

In no particular order, these risks can include:

1. *Market risk.*

    The state of the market is critical to the potential returns, and when you're in the development arena with up to a couple of years before the project is completed, you really need to understand not just where the market is when you invest, but where it's going. Ask yourself what stage of the property cycle the market is experiencing. If it's a boom situation and it has been for some time, it can be tempting to believe it can go on forever but be wary and listen to the experts.

2. *Is there demand?.*

    This is something that will be determined with some solid research. The developer needs to ensure that there's a market for the kind of dwellings you're planning in the area. For example, it's no use building affordable accommodation at the top end of town or building ritzy townhouses in a lower demographic area. They will look for the kind of businesses and services your market needs in the immediate area: transport, schools, shops (not boutiques), health and government services. If you get caught building a certain type of accommodation in an area where it's not wanted or needed, the research or advice is most likely to blame.

3. Delays.

Building is a notoriously difficult process to plan. You can have approval delays, materials shortages, weather delays, personnel problems, unreliable trades and site issues. Some of these can be hard to predict (like the weather), while others (like site issues such as geotechnical or soil remediation requirements) are discoverable through research. The way to mitigate these risks is to conduct your research, and to work with people who are experienced in negotiating the difficulties and delays that can beset (but rarely overwhelm) any property development.

4. Tenant risks.

If you're building to rent, the developer must consider tenant risks, and means taken to minimise them. That may be as simple as working with the right property managers in terms of skill, experience and local knowledge. There's a big difference between property managers that have just been assigned an area for the sake of tenanting out properties and those that are familiar with the area and the people.

5. Interest rates.

As I write, it has been over ten years since the RBA lifted the official interest rate in Australia[31], but inflation is on the rise for the first time in years and the pundits

*are factoring in an interest rate in mid to late 2022[32].
If you're borrowing to invest, you need to consider the
probability of interest rate rises and test your capacity
to accommodate them. Calculate your repayments with
rate increase increments of a quarter, half or even a full
one percent and be sure you can still cover them without
any additional income.*

6. *Gearing levels.*

   *If the developer is heavily geared, they are particularly
   vulnerable. The more that is borrowed, or the more the
   bank puts into the project, the riskier it is. Typically, on
   a property development there would be a 35% deposit
   and 65% would be borrowed. If the developer puts in
   10% and the bank has 90%, the risk is so much higher
   — should the value of the property go down, or interest
   rate rises affect the ability to service the debt, the bank
   may want to sell it to recoup their money, and no one
   else will have a say in the matter.*

There are undoubtedly other risks that I haven't included here,
and there will be area- or project-specific risks that you need
to anticipate. But a healthy dose of prudence, a modicum of
scepticism and a good deal of research will help mitigate the
risks involved.

What sort of projects should you invest in?

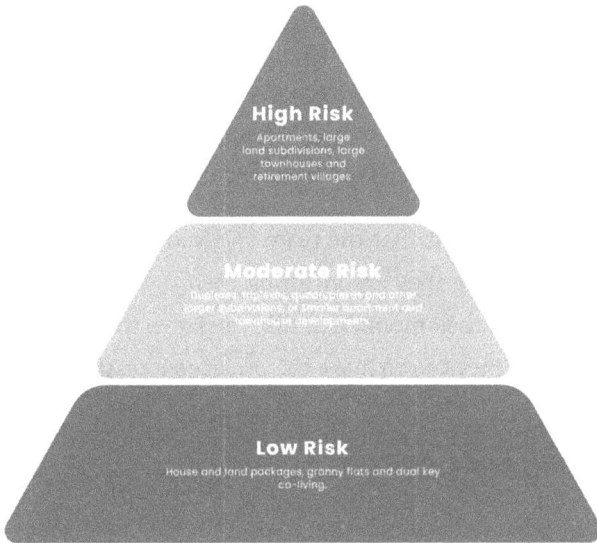

7. Risk-Reward Pyramid

Having determined your risk profile, considered the risks intrinsic to property investment and satisfied yourself of the developer's ability to eliminate, mitigate or tolerate them, it's time to seek out the project you will invest in. So what sort of projects are linked to different property development types?

+ *Low risk projects include house and land packages, granny flats and dual key co-living. The reason they are low risk is because they take a lower amount of capital to get involved or they're simpler projects.*

+ *Moderate risk developments can include duplexes, triplexes, quadruplexes and other larger subdivisions, or smaller apartment and townhouse developments.*

+ **High risk** projects are generally those entailing the design and construction of apartments, large land subdivisions, large townhouses and retirement villages.

Whatever investment type you choose, you need to be fully across what the details of the development are, and what the design, construction and management of the project will entail.

It's also important that the team involved have "skin in the game" meaning they are investing their own money alongside you — if their money is at risk, you know they'll be doing everything they can to make the project successful.

A final word on risk.

When you understand the risks and you take steps to manage them, you feel good about what you're doing. You have reserves, and you have control, perhaps not over the deal, but about how the deal impacts you. Stuff does and will happen, but it's how ready you are for it and how you handle it that matters.

The danger is that if you don't understand the project risk, you get a shock each time something happens and you become over-anxious. You lose sleep and you end up relying on others for your financial future, which means you're giving up your locus of control.

And that leads us into the final section in this chapter, which is about the importance of selecting developers and development teams that will give you as many tools as they can to understand and mitigate risks and recover from unavoidable mishaps.

Transparency and accountability.

One of the most effective ways of dealing with the risks associated with property investments is to work with people who have the requisite experience, a great track record, a collaborative approach and are open and honest communicators.

Mitigating the risk through transparency and accountability is the ultimate trust amplifier. Working with people you know you can trust, and being on the receiving end of regular, detailed communications, gives you peace of mind that you're more likely to have a good result.

An open and transparent developer? I'd like to see that.

Developers are notorious for playing their cards close to their chest. It seems that everything is on a "need to know" basis — and all the investor needs to know is that the developer is working on it.

When problems crop up, especially serious ones that can threaten the viability of the project, or at least result in costly delays, a lot of developers seem to get even more tight-lipped. Presumably, they don't want to worry, or worse, frighten their investors. Often the opposite effect to that intended is achieved — investors may view silence as an attempt to conceal a calamity.

But not all developers operate that way and your job is to go and find the ones that are open and accountable.

You can find these gems.

Given that the business environment is becoming more about transparency and accountability, not just to shareholders but to the wider community and our home planet — we've already talked about the UN Goals and B Corps — finding development teams or investing syndicates that tick all the boxes isn't as hard as it used to be. But I urge you not to accept anything at face value — do your homework and ensure that there's substance behind the persuasive marketing.

So how do you get to "see behind the curtain?"

When you're seeking a development pathway, look for a group or syndicate that provides monthly updates and gives you the ability to talk with the developer about the project whenever you need to. Bonus points are awarded if the group fosters networking with other investors and access to collaboration partners who will be equally transparent and accountable to you.

Property development has many moving parts, and things can and do go wrong, from missed deliveries and MIA tradies, to sudden market changes and interest rate rises. It's the developer's job to negotiate the project to a successful outcome in spite of all the challenges, and the good ones will do just that. But that doesn't mean you have to sit at home stewing in fear that everything will work out in the end.

As an investor, having visibility into the project means you know that the project is on track. The benefit of transparency is that it increases trust and makes repeat business more likely.

Here's an insight into why transparency works.

At High Impact Property Investments, we only work with developers who do regular Q&A webinars for our investor clients, which means:

✓ more engagement

✓ better relationships

✓ better ideas

Here's one example of how it's worked for us.

We worked with a particular developer on a commercial project and following completion, one of the units wasn't selling. Rather than brush it off or claim to have it in hand, the developers opened up about the issue at a monthly Q&A webinar call. The discussion became something of a brainstorm and the investors came up with some great ideas about how to position the unit to make it more appealing to the market. It was a superb example of the benefits of collaboration in action.

A sense of ownership.

When your developer operates like that and brings you into the solution, it gives you more of a sense of ownership. You don't just have money in it, you're investing your time and creativity and becoming emotionally involved in the success.

If you don't know what's happening, it's scary. You don't get enough warning when things go wrong and you get even more of a shock when problems become losses. Everyone we talk to has always agreed that they're more likely to work with a developer again when they are transparent because they like to be involved and engaged. And we know from experience that our investors are much more likely to trust the developer to overcome problems if they've been informed and included all the way through.

Don't let the risks overwhelm you.

There's been a lot of talk in this chapter about risk, and it's not a subject we can or should avoid. Because there's no escaping the fact that risk and returns are inextricably linked. You will have to take risks if you're going to get returns.

And while we're talking about returns, never lose sight of the potential rewards. The financial benefits to you can be very pleasing, and the benefits to the wider community can be extraordinary.

So my advice to you is not to let fear get the better of you. Understand the risks and create strategies to minimise or eliminate them as much as possible. Work with people you can trust to overcome the problems that will arise on any project. And get involved. Mutual understanding, trust and collaboration are the keys to success — and that is the ideal place to move on to our next chapter, C is for Collaboration.

For a special video relating to investment risk visit:

https://www.hipi.global/book/investmentrisk

Chapter 8

C is for Collaboration.

As the world becomes more specialised and each of us cultivates our own niche of talents and skills, the need for collaboration grows.

Solving the big social issues isn't going to happen by a bunch of individuals — however talented and creative — sitting in their silos thinking about it. The big solutions we need are going to come from collaboration across numerous disciplines and spheres, because the problems themselves are multi-disciplinary. A physicist alone can't solve climate change, any more than a developer alone can make a ten-storey apartment building appear. It takes massive levels of cooperation, mutual trust, and extraordinary commitment to communication and accountability.

Let me tell you (another) story.

My first affordable housing project is something I am really proud of but the process was something of a baptism of fire. The builder went broke, I fell out with my joint venture partner and the stress was so high I began to question whether I should be in property development at all.

I was feeling pretty raw, and it seemed that the answer would be to work on my own, rather than take on joint venture partners. If I could rely on no one but myself, then that's what I would do. Because the one thing I knew was that I desperately wanted to create more affordable homes.

In order to prepare myself, I attended a number of personal development workshops. I wanted to better understand myself, my personal motivations and my relationships with money. That way I could go out and achieve my goals without getting into messy relationships and trusting people who shouldn't be trusted.

But then something happened. During one of those workshops, part of the course was a group challenge — a difficult and at times seemingly impossible task (I can't tell you what it was because it's confidential but suffice to say it was tough). What I noticed while mired in the task was that when I felt like it was all too hard and that we would never get through it, my teammates were there to pick me up and push me through. Then, when others had lost their buoyancy and were in danger of being over-come by the challenge, I was able to help them through it.

Eventually, after many hours, a huge burden of stress and a rollercoaster ride that took all of us from the depths of despair to the heights of elation, we successfully completed the challenge.

I learned a lot from that experience, but the single most valuable thing it taught me was that I really needed to collaborate with others. I found that when I do cooperate and work as part of a team, the job gets easier, the load gets lighter and the rewards somehow seem brighter.

Meeting Symon.

Shortly after that, I met Symon Peters, whom you will remember from Chapter 5 — T is for Track Record. Symon invited me to collaborate with 360 Collective, which brings together all of the specialists, professionals, key players and on-the-ground personnel necessary to create high quality property developments. I realised that if life was better working with a team, then this was the kind of crew I should be working with. By joining a multi-disciplinary team, I could stick to my area of expertise, which is raising funds and not try to wear all those other hats at the same time.

Why you should collaborate and what you need to know.

High impact property investment is a complex and demanding field. It requires top level expertise from a wide array of people across a sometimes-bewildering array of disciplines. Behind the people who immediately spring to mind — like architects, builders, landscapers, real estate agents and development managers — there is an extended line of people with very specific skillsets and experience. Each of them needs to do their job well, and all of their contributions need to be carefully coordinated. The logistics alone are frightening and the potential for trouble is magnified by the sheer number of connections, co-dependencies and relationships.

The need for collaboration is obvious and paramount to success.

The developer is the linchpin.

A good property investment syndicate is led by an experienced, accomplished developer — a skilled and intuitive leader who can pull all the team members together both internally and externally. You need to be sure that the team you choose to work with has that strength of leadership and that it is incorporated with strong internal development team and external collaboration teams — each of which is only as strong as its weakest link.

Communication is the key.

When you think about it, collaboration is almost entirely about transparency and accountability — with a bit of openness to creativity, the sharing of ideas and a strong basis of cooperation thrown in.

As an investor, you choose your team on their experience, track record and alignment with your values. Your research into those factors is critical to selecting the right team. The final test they must pass, as I discussed in the previous chapter on risk, is that of transparency and accountability.

But if there's no communication, you don't know if the team will deliver the development to a successful conclusion. If you don't know exactly how collaborative and communicative a team really is, you're investing in the dark.

On the other hand, when you know who the team are and what they can achieve through collaboration, you'll be much more comfortable and be able to confidently predict success without the stress that not knowing brings.

The roles of the collaboration partners.

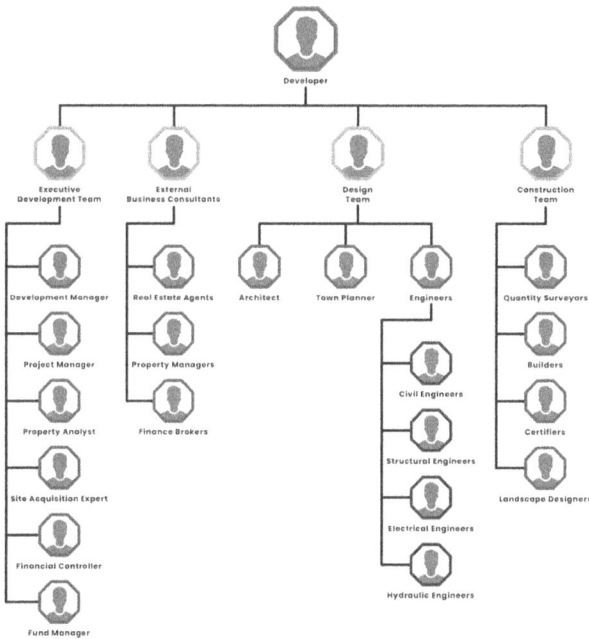

8. A *Typical Property Development Team*

A high impact property development is a delicate balancing act, and one that demands patience, expertise and a massive amount of communication and collaboration.

There are a lot of different people with different qualifications, modes of work, skills and experience involved in taking a property development from an idea to an accomplishment. The bigger and more complex the project, the larger the team will become.

While a smaller development may be fine with a development manager or project manager working on their own, for instance, on a larger project those people are likely to have teams working under them. The same applies for people working in the various engineering disciplines, the design and fitout, and so on.

Clearly, with larger projects the building team not only grows, the list of plant and equipment required on site increases as well — there are more concrete and cement trucks and workers, scaffolding and scaffolders, cranes and crane operators and an assortment of other heavy and light machinery along with their respective operators.

But there is a core team of people at the head of the organisation whose job it is to develop the idea, ensure that it is viable, drive it through the design and approval stages, ensure it is executed to the standards required, and follow through with sales, settlements and the distribution of profits. These we can call the executive development team, and their numbers will include the:

✦ *Developer — the mastermind behind the whole deal, the developer is someone whose knowledge of the property market, design, building and management has led them to the idea in the first place. Their job is to find property investment opportunities and maximise the reality that they build out of each opportunity they seize. The developer's desk is where the buck stops and all complaints and major issues will end up there. A good developer understands technical matters ranging from finance to geology to building materials and is an expert at managing people, finding creative solutions to problems, soothing spooked investors, assuring finance providers, and presenting the public relations face of the project. The bigger the project, the bigger the task of the developer.*

✦ *Development Manager — the job of the development manager is to ensure that the whole job runs as smoothly as possible, taking care of disruptions, problems and personnel issues while overseeing the marketing, sales and other aspects of delivery. Their job begins with organising the funding and continues through the purchase of the site, the construction and everything through to sales and settlement. The development manager is also responsible for coordinating the rest of the executive development team.*

✦ *Project Manager — usually someone with a depth of experience in building and construction, the project manager oversees the construction of the development from start to finish. Their job ranges from supervising the transformation of designs into detailed drawings and specifications, to liaison with the builders and suppliers, creating and administering logistics and timelines and ensuring that quality control standards are met.*

✦ *Property Analyst — this crucial role is all about determining whether the deal stacks up for the developer, the investors and the people who will live in the development. At the outset, the analyst crunches the numbers and assesses whether or not there is a strong business case. This will include sifting through a lot of data around the location and the site, from market conditions and demographics to setting budgets and financial projections, administering the legal aspects surrounding the development and even setting the lease conditions.*

✦ *Site Acquisition Expert — tasked with selecting, vetting and researching potential sites for development, site acquisition experts negotiate the pricing and the deal, and liaise with the real estate agents regarding the purchase.*

✦ *Financial Controller — the person who takes care of the day-to-day bookkeeping and accounting, and the running project costs. This includes operating and monitoring bank accounts, the daily, weekly and monthly disbursements, reconciliations and taxation compliance.*

✦ *Fund Manager — in property investment syndicates, the fund manager is the person who will deal most with investors, and their role is to communicate the scope, intentions and design outcomes of the project to those investors, and to manage the investor funds. One of their primary responsibilities is to ensure that the investment process complies with the Australian Financial Services Regulations.*

On the next level of experts involved in the project, there will usually be all or most of the following external consultants or businesses:

✦ *Real Estate Agents — getting involved at the start, with the purchase of the site, and at the end, with the sale of the properties, real estate agents handle the commercial part of the transaction, including coordinating the settlement agents and compliance issues such as stamp duty and managing funds in trust.*

✦ *Property Managers — in rental situations, the property or rental managers work with the development manager to organise the marketing for the finished property, run the tenant selection process, and collect bonds and advance rent and place them in trust accounts. Once the tenants are in residence, the property managers collect the rent, carry out inspections, and deal with any problems or issues that arise for the tenants. Often the real estate agents involved above will also act as the property manager, but the individual owners have the option to choose their own rental management team.*

✦ *Finance brokers — where private or bank finance is required, the finance broker will research the finance deals available and select a shortlist for the development team. Once the finance type is approved, they will liaise with the finance providers and negotiate the deal.*

Then there is what we might call the building team — the people responsible for creating the design and getting the project built, fitted out and ready to move in. This team ranges from highly qualified professionals to the labourers who will carry out the construction work — meet the:

✦ *Architect — starting with a concept originated to meet the developer's brief, the architect creates the overall look and style of the building and everything in it, from light fittings and floor coverings to building materials, as well as items like balustrades, cladding styles and even effects like murals.*

✦ *Town Planner — managing the process of getting the development approval through council is a specialist task and the town planner needs to have a firm grip on the local, state and national codes.*

✦ *Engineering professionals — depending on the size and complexity of the project, some or all of these engineers and their associated personnel will be required:*

✦ *Civil engineers to take care of earthworks and other civil inclusions such as paths and roads, carparks and drainage.*

✦ *Structural engineers to interpret the architectural draw-ings and ensure that the structural design of the building conforms to those drawings, designing the underlying structure to ensure it has the strength and durability to stand up to the pressures of human traffic, wind, weather, seismic events and other tests of its integrity.*

❖ Electrical engineers to arrange for the power to site while construction is under way, and design and install all electrical fittings, which these days also includes data cabling.

❖ Hydraulics engineers to provide the requisite water to the site and if necessary also consult on inclusions such as lifts and escalators.

❖ Quantity surveyors — working from the detailed design drawings, the quantity surveyors are essentially external to the project (often completing due diligence/verifications on behalf of the bank). They calculate the type and volume of materials needed and keep track of the costs and expenses of the project throughout.

❖ Builders — the concrete workers, bricklayers, carpenters, plumbers, electricians, glaziers, floor and window covering installers and other trades that turn plans into reality.

❖ Certifiers — the inspectors who are responsible for ensuring that the construction meets the relevant building codes. They must be familiar with those codes and be able to read and interpret the detailed drawings to ensure that all internal fittings, from concrete reinforcement to joists, footings and other structural elements, are all as per the specification.

❖ Landscape designers — the final touch to the development is the landscape design, and this demands a professional who is able to create a look and feel that

> *is commensurate with the building design. In addition,*
> *the landscape designer ensures that the exterior spaces*
> *are functional and conducive to community amenity*
> *and that the flora used meet with local planning codes.*

That's a lot of people — it literally takes a village...

You begin to see the vast complexity of this business, and the intricacy of the relationships between each of the many working parts. Problems in one area can cascade and create other problems further down the line, so it really pays to have a strong team that works well together and understands each other.

Where the team isn't as strong as it can be, you'll most often find that it contains some consultants that just treat it as a job, without getting as involved as they should. This means they have to be chased up a lot and if they're not passionate about it you can get left at the bottom of the pile. That can be very stressful, and it can have a negative effect on the outcome.

Price can be a big factor.

When you're working on a property development, particularly one in which you are keen for the final product to be affordable but also comfortable and amenable, the temptation is to save money wherever you can. But beware — choosing your team by price can be very expensive in the end.

In my own experience, I've worked on a development in which there was a lot of pressure on the builder, from one of our JV partners, to reduce their prices and do the job at the lowest possible cost. But what that meant was they weren't invested in the job, they didn't want to spend extra time making it right, and the whole thing ended up being incredibly difficult for everyone. Then the builder went broke anyway.

So where you can, choose your consultants and team members for their ability and their passion rather than just looking at the number at the bottom of the page. Don't try to "save money" by using people or teams that will end up costing you big time.

Final check: Do you value their values?

On top of all the above, which I admit is a lot to take in, you need to choose a team that meets one very special requirement: their values need to align with yours. It's a topic by itself, and one that doesn't really belong in a discussion about collaboration, so it warrants an entire chapter of its own. Read on!

For a special video relating to collaboration visit:
https://www.hipi.global/book/collaboration

SCAN ME

A is for Aligned Values.

The bridge that can connect your purpose to the long-term benefits derived by others is constructed from a composite of your values and the values of those with whom you partner. It is important to understand and adhere to both.

Once upon a time, the prevailing sentiment in the investment community was to just make money and not worry too much about how. Hey, if I don't invest in that tobacco company/uranium mine/textile company that uses slave labour, someone else will, right?

But in the first twenty years of the 21st century (at least), there's been a dramatic shift in consciousness. As I've already pointed out numerous times in this book, there's a burgeoning realisation that the solution to the problems of the world is the same as the cause — and that is us. We, the people.

And along with that realisation has come a shift in actions, too, as we realise that we can make money by doing good things, rather than ignoring what effect our investments have on the community and the environment. As a consequence of this global awakening, we now have much greater levels of transparency and choice when considering where and how to invest our money.

Purpose based investing has become a "thing", and its relevance and importance is growing faster and faster as the idea catches on.

It pays to invest time into clarifying your values.

9. What do you most value?

What are your values? It's not an easy question to answer unless you've examined the issue before and been able to articulate what your values are. But it's critical to the process of figuring out how to identify people who may be a good fit to work with and auditing their values to make sure that a good fit is in fact a very snug and comfortable one.

That's why I so strongly advocate a values self-audit.

Before you can "values audit" someone else, you need to have explored and articulated your own values. When you've taken the time and trouble do that, it helps you gain clarity over what to invest in and why, and you make better investment decisions. But it also allows you to compare other peoples' values with your own and see where there's overlap and where there are gaps. If those gaps are insurmountable, the deal really should be off the table.

Now, this isn't a general self-help book, so I am not going to go into detail about your values across your whole life — although I certainly would not discourage you from conducting a complete values self-audit. If you do that, it will inform our present discussion and you'll find out more about yourself. And if you want to, there are plenty of places online where you can ask yourself values-related questions such as:

- ✦ *What makes you happy?*

- ✦ *What are you most proud of in your life?*

- ✦ *What makes you angry?*

✦ *What social issues do you think are the most important for we as a society to tackle first?*

Some sites will give you lists of up to several hundred values-related words and ask you to choose five.

But I digress. This book is about high impact property investing, so focus on your values as they relate to this topic. Here are 8 simple questions that will help you:

1. *Do you think that affordable housing, sustainable building, building resilient communities and creating specialist disability accommodation is a good idea?*

2. *Do you think vulnerable people should have the opportunity to own their own homes, or to rent places they can afford rather than couch surf or live in cars?*

3. *Do you think it's "someone else's" job to make that happen, or is it up to people like you and me?*

4. *Rate these outcomes in order of your preference:*

   a. *Benefits to deserving individuals*

   b. *Environmental advantages*

   c. *Financial reward*

   d. *Social benefits*

5. *If given the choice between building an affordable housing project using sustainable methods, or a chic, expensive but non-sustainably built development — and both had the same potential returns — which one would you choose?*

6. *If the projected financial return on an affordable and sustainable development was slightly lower than a competing project, but still in double digits, which would you choose?*

7. *Are you prepared to invest a little more of your own energy and time to ensure an outcome that has a positive effect on the people who will live in the development, the environment and the community at large?*

8. *Do you think auditing the values of people you are considering working with is just too much like hard work?*

Yes, these are closed questions but keep an open mind because your answers may well confirm that you are indeed, reading the right book at the right time to put your values to work.

Finding out down the track may be too late.

Not so long ago I got involved in a joint venture with a partner who had a piece of land suitable for an eco-affordable housing development. He had a lot of experience and I could see that this was something sorely needed in the community, so I was really excited about the prospect of working with him. Like most people, I hadn't at that stage really addressed the issue of what my values are, but I had a vague idea, and I thought that was enough. The concept of the project was good and I must admit, I was very impressed with the connections that he had — he was a bit of a mover and shaker — and I thought he was really going places. So I went into it willingly.

As the weeks went on, it began to dawn on me that my values and the developer's values were not actually aligned, even though I'd been led to believe they were. Red flags kept cropping up everywhere until there were just too many to ignore.

Fortunately, we were able to part ways before we got too deep into the project but I had lost a lot of valuable time and could easily have lost money as well.

The lesson out of that was to do a values audit before getting involved with someone. Importantly, my gut feeling from the outset was that there was something — I couldn't put my finger on it — that just wasn't right about his approach. So I also vowed to listen to those gut feelings in the future.

And that's an interesting situation because as I've said throughout this book, you need to let logic be your guide and be careful not to make emotional decisions but in that case, I had the opportunity to make an important distinction between emotion and discernment — perhaps you could call it an educated gut feeling. I guess you could say I'm backtracking here, but the difference is that my gut was telling me about the person rather than the project — I wasn't letting emotion rule me in regard to the property investment itself.

Look before you leap.

If you're very focused on a goal, or an opportunity comes along that is so attractive it can blind you to everything else. That's when you can become quite vulnerable to making emotional decisions that may come back to bite you. And only when your vision clears will you know, almost instantly, that you've made a poor choice. So be careful.

If you stand for nothing, what will you fall for? *

If you choose not to be a part of the global movement — spending and investing for good — I am not going to judge you. But whatever happens I urge you to consider your values before you invest in anything.

When your values aren't aligned with what you're investing in or with the team involved, you'll feel unsettled. Like me, you may not be able to put your finger on it, but that will only make it worse because you just won't feel comfortable.

When that happens, you can get mixed results at best and the whole process seems harder and more stressful. You're not having fun and it's not as good as it could be. Worse, if you've gotten past the point of no return and you have to stick with it, it can be a drag on your whole life. Even if it's a financial success, you won't feel very successful.

*Line pinched from *Hamilton: An American Musical*. (Thanks)

Here's how to be sure your values align.

Aligned values mean that you can trust that everyone is pulling in the same direction — willingly. That's more important than you may realise.

There's no easy way to values-audit someone else. They could be saying the right things, and in the courtship phase even the least sincere of hucksters can be charming and persuasive. But if you just accept a developer's word that they're on the same page as you, you could be disappointed later, when it's much more difficult to extricate yourself. So what you need to do is examine their actions.

Quickly find the best answers by boldly asking the right questions.

What does any developer you're considering working with stand for? What is their purpose? How are they contributing? Look for evidence that they are providing access to affordable, inclusive, sustainable housing, rather than just marketing statements. Ask them to show you how they're building resilient communities. Ask if they are contributing outside of their developments and what examples they can give.

If you find development teams or syndicates can answer all your questions and provide the proof to back it up, you know they're in it to make the world a better place. But keep going. Quiz them about charitable donations. Ask them if they're aware of the UN Global Sustainable Development Goals, B Corps, and B1G1. Closer to home, do they invest time in improving their team, and their community? Is their team itself inclusive and diverse?

Actions speak louder than words so assess their actions.

When a mining company blew up a sacred cave in 2020, that one action spoke louder than all the platitudes and empty slogans they'd been spouting for years about how much they care about people, and environment, and Indigenous culture and heritage. So always see if a development team's actions match their words.

Different organisations and syndicates are attracted to providing affordable homes because they can get good returns on it but when profit is the primary motive and it's not balanced by care for people and the environment, then decisions are made on profit only. As previously suggested, you may not be comfortable with profit as the lone motivation and driver.

You'll be glad you checked, so make sure you do.

When you invest with teams that don't align with your values, one way or another, sooner or later, you'll feel bad about it. Because you won't be able to escape the fact that instead of making the world a better place you're actually contributing to its deterioration, if not destruction. You could be setting a poor example for your kids and you could be proving to people that your values are only as deep as your pockets.

On the other hand, when you and your team are all working to make the world a better place, even a small contribution will help the community, help the wider society, and help the world we live on. Believe me, you will feel good about it because you're leaving a legacy.

So, let's finish this book with one more substantive chapter, the one that wraps up why your legacy is so important.

For a special video relating to aligned values visit:

https://www.hipi.global/book/alignedvalues

Chapter 10

L is for Legacy.

10. My First Affordable Housing Project,
Ocean Shores (Completed 2018)

Photo supplied by Futurewood Pty Ltd, supplier of the composite
cladding, screening and decking used on this project

Throughout this book, I've been at pains to emphasise how important it is to make property investments rationally and without undue emotion. But it's time to admit it: this is an emotional business.

The thrill I get every time I walk or drive past my first affordable housing development has never faded or diminished in any way — every single time I feel the glow of pride and happiness about what I helped to create. In almost four years since the people who live there moved in — including three who pay 80% of the market rate in rent (and will do for ten years) — their lives have settled and new possibilities have opened up for them.

That's what building a legacy is about. The kind of change that we can make is astonishing when you think about it — especially when you consider that the financial return for the investors in that project was 25% per annum.

Just imagine for a moment, that you could help build the answers to these questions:

✦ *What would life be like if we created more accessible housing so that people living with disabilities or older people were able to really live and express themselves in their homes? What would the improved health outcomes do for our healthcare and welfare systems? Our justice system? Our overall economy?*

✦ *How much more vibrant would our neighbourhoods be with such an incredible diversity of people? Especially since so many of whom would be so much closer to reaching their potential — the self-actualisation envisioned by Abraham Maslow eighty or so years ago.*

✦ *What would it be like not just to build more resilient communities but to live in one? To make your home in a place where you feel welcomed and valued, where your neighbours have your back and you feel safe every day. To share community gardens and to be able to simply stop and have a chat with your neighbours, who are also your friends. To know that if something went wrong, the whole community would be there to help you through it, and to know that you'd be there for your neighbours when they were at their most vulnerable.*

✦ *How much waste could we save if more of us switched to building modular housing? If we all maximised our reliance on renewable energy, how much greenhouse gas emission could we reduce? How much less pollution would there be?*

These are not just dreams. They're a reality that's waiting in the wings, for people like you and me to bring into existence. And that's why building a legacy is so vitally important — for the difference it can make not just to your life, but to the lives of so many people around you and indeed to the environment and the planet itself.

The investment benefits of building a legacy.

The financial benefits of high impact property investments are by now well established. As noted above, my first affordable housing project produced results of 25% per annum, and this is not unusual.

As I write, we are deep into a big project that will deliver affordable rooming accommodation to 72 residents on completion in June 2023. Designed to provide affordable living for young professionals and women over 55 years, the project, in Loganlea in Queensland, will return an average room rental $265 — $285 per week. That will give investors a healthy projected financial return of around 20% per annum.

However, the social and environmental benefits of the project are also outstanding. It's within walking distance to shops and amenities including public transport nearby, which reduces the need for vehicular travel. The design is oriented to make the most of solar access to the building in winter and passive cooling in summer. And facilities include shared cars and bikes. To cap it off, the building is designed for net zero emissions, and there's a community garden that creates an interactive and productive meeting place.

For a project that will deliver such an attractive financial return, the positive social and environmental impacts are exceptional. But this project also illustrates one of the great advantages of choosing to create a lasting legacy by investing in high impact projects.

Creating a legacy changes your perspective.

Think about what it means to build a legacy. You begin to assess potential investments not purely from their financial angle, but from a wider viewpoint. Suddenly, how the project will affect your family's future, the cohesiveness of our community and the sustainability of our current quality of life, becomes important.

You instinctively shift from accepting mediocrity or one-dimensional dollar-focused thinking, to seeking projects that will stand the test of time. You look for developments that will improve society and help stabilise our climate and environment. Rather than just the payday — which remains important — you focus on creating something you would be proud to point out to your family, friends and future generations.

It's a deliberate and conscious change in your mode of thinking that actually helps you make better investment decisions. Besides that, it will give you the:

✓ **resolve to do the work** *to ensure that your development team's values align with yours and that their experience and track record are appropriate to the task(s) ahead.*

✓ **courage to make big decisions** *because you know that they are the right decisions.*

✓ **opportunities to meet the right people** *who share your vision for a better world. People who will inspire you and be inspired by you. You'll spur each other on and you'll have fun doing great work.*

I know, because I've done it.

Start today.

The construction industry is one of the biggest sources of greenhouse gases and waste on our fragile globe. The buildings we invest in need to be built, there's no getting around that — particularly those with a positive social impact. But they don't have to be as damaging and short-lived as they are currently.

We have the tools, the technology and the skills to build in such a way that the buildings we create help us to thrive while reducing the impact the construction process and the ongoing use of those buildings will have on the planet.

What many of us lack is the will and the motivation. Too many of us don't see the urgency. But the need for change is indeed critically pressing.

The International Panel on Climate Change says we have at the most ten years before climate change becomes irreversible. So the need for taking action to reduce the environmental impact of everything we do — especially in activities like building that create such ruinous levels of waste — is imperative.

On a social level, the inequality gap is getting wider all the time. The number of marginalised people is growing and with their increasing number the problems and costs of poverty — the healthcare burden, crime statistics, substance abuse and anti-social behaviour, education failure and unemployment — multiply. And none of us is immune to those impacts.

We need to start thinking long term and making a commitment to building a legacy is a crucial part of that. If you don't consider your legacy, you may be making short term decisions that can negatively affect us all. Not pursuing a legacy can lead to inaction when action is required.

More good news — it's not difficult.

Making the change is as easy as asking yourself what legacy you want to leave. Do you want to pass on a better world than the one you came into? Do you care enough about your fellow humans and the coming generations to make a few small changes? Remember, I am not asking you to make any massive financial sacrifices, just to change your thinking a little.

When you've thought a little about your preferred legacy, ask yourself how close you are you to delivering that legacy. Look at where you are now and consider what actions you need to take to get where you want to be.

Consider how high impact property investing can contribute to achieving your goals. It will provide you with a financial heritage that you can pass on to your family, while making a positive impact on the lives of perhaps hundreds or even thousands of people. It will give you living, indelible evidence of how you have been true to your values and acted to pass them on to others. Every day you'll be able to say, with pride and humility, "I did that. I made the world a better place, and I learned how energising and rewarding making a difference can be."

For a special video relating to legacy
visit: https://www.hipi.global/book/legacy

SCAN ME

It's up to you now.

Writing this book has been an amazing experience for me. It has helped to clarify a lot of my thoughts and beliefs around high impact property investments and strengthened my conviction that it is the right way to approach a potentially profitable venture.

Since I started on the high impact property investment journey, I've made my share of mistakes and taken a few wrong turns but along the way I've gathered a lot of valuable knowledge and experience. I've also managed to develop an amazing network of people who also believe in the potential of high impact property investment to change the world. Yes, the changes we all make may only make a ripple when we make them but then again, there's a thing called the ripple effect — and that's what can end up affecting a world of difference.

I created the ETHICAL framework so I could share my experience with people who are part of or are exploring the global movement demonstrating the power of doing business for good.

We've talked about the importance of experience and track record in selecting your investments and your development team. We've examined the potential positive impacts your participation in high impact investments can have, and we've acknowledged the risks involved. We also discussed the ways to mitigate or eliminate those risks, often relating back to our reliance on experience and track record.

The make-up of a development team and the importance of collaboration took up an entire chapter and we followed that with a discourse on how to ensure that your collaborators' values are aligned with your own. And we finished on a more emotional, even spiritual note, with an essay about the importance of creating a legacy.

We have covered a great deal of ground and in many ways, we've only scratched the surface. The one thing that is indispensable in this business is experience, and the only way to gain that is to get out there and actually invest.

But the beauty of experience is that it's cumulative, and the more you get involved, the more you learn and the greater your confidence will be. My network is now developing a $14 million property that will give 72 residents an opportunity to meet their own potential, and that's incredible. But I started much smaller than that because I had to learn the ropes. I had to make the mistakes.

Having made those mistakes, built the network I now have

and written this book, I'm allowing you to skip a few steps. You can leverage off my experience just by reading these words and use the ETHICAL framework to kickstart your own development team. I really don't mind if you do that because the important thing here is the work. Australia needs more affordable housing, a more sustainable design and building approach, more resilient communities, and more specialist disability accommodation, and there's more than enough opportunity coming down the pipe for all of us.

Otherwise, if you wish, you can leverage off the experience of my team and join the High Impact Property Investment network, which means you can go straight to the big, important and higher impact projects. As long as you bring the right values and attitude to the group, you'll always be welcome.

In fact, as far as I'm concerned, anyone and everyone who gets into this business for the right reasons, not just to make money but to improve our world, is more than welcome — you belong.

Next Steps

There are several resources available to help you on your journey to ETHICAL Property Investing.

ETHICAL Property Investing Scorecard

We have designed a measurement tool to help you assess how ready you are to make double digit returns through ethical property investment.

Before you read on, take the ETHICAL Property Investing scorecard at **https://www.hipi.global/scorecard**

This set of questions is designed to score you on the 7 areas that make up the ETHICAL Framework described in this book. It gives you a customised report based on your answers.

The results of the scorecard will give you a starting point and show you where you are already strong and where you need to focus your attention.

https://www.hipi.global/scorecard

High Impact Property Investment Network

Our High Impact Property Investor Network is ideal for busy professionals that want their money to work for them, in a way that contributes to society and is in alignment with their values. The network delivers investment opportunities to members, which are run by experienced developers dedicated to creating ethical property investments with a high degree of accountability and transparency.

HIPI) HIGH IMPACT
PROPERTY
INVESTMENTS

Find out more, visit **https://www.hipi.global/network**

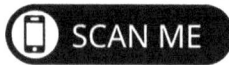

SCAN ME

Join The Movement

If this book has inspired you and you would like to support the work we do at High Impact Property Investments, I invite you and your friends to post your thoughts, testimonials and acknowledgements about ETHICAL property investing on our social media channels.

www.linkedin.com/company/ high-impact-property-investments

www.facebook.com/highimpactproperty.investments/

www.instagram.com/highimpactproperty.investments/

Acknowledgements

I extend special thanks to Symon Peters and the team at 360 Collective for reminding me of the power of collaboration. Thank you, Symon for encouraging me to burn the ships and go for it.

To my girlfriends Laurie, Pam, Sarah, Jen and Mel, I honour our commitment to sisterhood for the past 12 years. Thank you for growing with me.

To the team and community at Dent Global, thank you for helping me to redefine what was possible for myself and my business, clarify my message and get it out to as many people as possible.

To Lucy McCarraher and Joe Gregory of Rethink Press, thank you for the encouragement to start this book. To Marlon "Train" Forrester of Line and Length and Luke Harris of Working Type Studio, a big thank you to you and your team for the technical skills to get it published.

To my team at High Impact Property Investments; Ant, Michelle, Karen, Amelia and Charmaine, I really appreciate you. Let's rock this!

To Eric and Sue, thank you for being so supportive and loving, and for starting us on this journey.

To Patricia and Glen, thank you for your love and the way you made me. I wouldn't change a single thing.

To Ant, Mahlia and Atticus, you are my greatest inspiration in life. Thank you for being you and letting me be me.

And finally, to my fellow HIPI's — whether you are investors past or present, have provided encouragement and support during the making of this book, or are part of the movement to make ethical property investing the norm and not the exception, thank you for your faith and trust in me.

With much appreciation

Dionne
February 2022

#proudtobeahipi

The Author

Dr. Dionne Payn is the Founder and CEO of High Impact Property Investments. The company specialises in partnering investors looking for double digit returns with projects that provide affordable and sustainable homes.

Dionne has a PhD in Natural Products Chemistry, has project managed a number of property developments in New South Wales, Australia and has helped almost 40 investors to achieve double digit returns through property. These property projects range from small one into two subdivisions up to larger co-living projects.

Dionne's first taste of ethical property development came in 2017 / 2018, when she project managed a 14-townhouse project. This development delivered affordable rental and owner-occupied homes in an area well known for its high level of housing un-affordability.

The experience of being financially well rewarded for this project while providing affordable homes for low to moderate income earners was a game-changer and led to her drive to make a difference to people's lives through property.

Dionne's goal is to raise $1 billion by December 2026 for projects that provide affordable homes, sustainable properties, build resilient communities and provide accessible homes for people with disabilities.

She believes that through social enterprise and private investment we can transform lives and end homelessness, particularly in vulnerable women and children.

Endnotes

1   http://websites.umich.edu/~thecore/doc/Friedman.pdf

2   https://www.nielsen.com/wp-content/uploads/sites/3/2019/04/global-sustainability-report.pdf

3   https://www.businessinsider.com.au/millennials-are-driving-a-huge-shift-in-the-way-we-shop-and-invest-2018-5?r=US&IR=T

4   https://www.afr.com/property/australia-will-need-1-million-more-social-affordable-homes-by-2036-20190312-h1cb89

5   https://aware.com.au/content/dam/ftc/digital/pdfs/about/media/2019/2019.07.08%20%20Affordable%20Housing%20-%20First%20State%20Super%20leads%20in%20Affordable%20Housing.pdf

6   https://www.afr.com/property/commercial/aware-super-backs-300-million-affordable-housing-project-20210209-p570up

7   https://themarketherald.com.au/federal-government-sells-first-sustainable-housing-bond-for-343-million-2021-05-31/

8   https://www.afr.com/property/commercial/2-5b-disability-housing-sector-set-to-explode-in-size-20210817-p58jdo

9   https://aifs.gov.au/facts-and-figures/population-and-households

10 https://profile.id.com.au/australia/bedrooms

11 https://www.ndis.gov.au/providers/housing-and-living-supports-and-services/specialist-disability-accommodation/sda-demand-data

12 https://www.abs.gov.au/statistics/health/disability/disability-ageing-and-carers-australia-summary-findings/2018

13 https://en.wikipedia.org/wiki/Free_range

14 https://sdgs.un.org/goals

15 https://www.bcorporation.com.au/

16 https://www.gensler.com

17 https://www.businessinsider.com.au/australia-housing-market-his-toric-price-cycles-2018-4

18 https://www.ato.gov.au/About-ATO/Research-and-statistics/In-de-tail/Taxation-statistics/Taxation-statistics-2018-19/?anchor=Individ-ualsstatistics#Table7Individuals

19 https://www.perthnow.com.au/business/staggering-cost-of-dooms-day-scenario-on-australian-economy-c-4985966

20 https://www.theguardian.com/australia-news/2021/jan/20/austra-lian-housing-system-broken-with-more-than-half-of-low-income-renters-facing-rental-stress

21 https://www.abs.gov.au/statistics/economy/price-indexes-and-infla-tion/residential-property-price-indexes-eight-capital-cities/latest-re-lease

22 https://thebigissue.org.au/news/the-value-of-a-home-benefits-of-permanent-housing/

23 https://www.unifiedlawyers.com.au/blog/global-divorce-rates-statis-tics/

24 https://www.architectureanddesign.com.au/news/1m-social-and-af-fordable-homes-needed-by-2036

25 https://theconversation.com/buildings-produce-25-of-austra-lias-emissions-what-will-it-take-to-make-them-green-and-wholl-pay-105652

26 https://www.aph.gov.au/About_Parliament/Parliamentary_Depart-ments/Parliamentary_Library/pubs/BriefingBook46p/CostLiving

27 https://dcfw.org/the-triangle-swindon/

28 https://data.ndis.gov.au/media/2827/download?attachment

29 SDA 2020-21 quarter 4 report

30 https://www.apra.gov.au/financial-claims-scheme-0

31 https://www.infochoice.com.au/rate-watch/history-of-inter-est-rate-movements/

32 https://www.smh.com.au/politics/federal/economists-tip-august-in-terest-rate-hike-as-the-cost-of-living-rises-20220124-p59qoc.html

www.ingramcontent.com/pod-product-compliance
Lightning Source LLC
Chambersburg PA
CBHW071234210326
41597CB00016B/2042